Inspiring Women

True Confidence

Wendy Bray

Published 2008 by CWR, Waverley Abbey House, Waverley Lane, Farnham, Surrey GU9 8EP, UK. Registered Charity No. 294387. Registered Limited Company No. 1990308.

See back of book for list of National Distributors.

Concept development, editing, design and production by CWR

Cover image: Getty Images/Stone/Zubin Shroff

Printed in Finland by WS Bookwell

ISBN: 978-1-85345-470-7

Contents

Acknowledgements

A special 'Thank you' to …

Steve – for boldly saying what needed to be said (as ever!)
The 'ladies' of St Nic's Newbury – for sharing their weekend with me
Teena – for being the best of friends
Carol – for her thoughtful and gracious editing
And Lynette and Sue – for being bold enough to encourage the path of adventure God has started us on with this book!

Introduction

Sometimes a book contains a story – occasionally it becomes part of one.

As I began writing this book, I had no idea that I was embarking on a personal adventure. As I explain a little later, in Chapter One, the subject matter in itself is a challenge for me. But even as I began to write the first chapter, I had no idea how the book itself, or the longer 'story' it echoes, would end.

I didn't know that the material God had inspired me to write would do more than give women something to read and think about: that it would change lives, prompt women to take action in their communities and become the context in which the Holy Spirit would move with grace, tenderness and power. But God knew: He is a God of surprises.

My sense of inadequacy has been packed up in a metaphorical suitcase as I have been taken on both a personal quest and a shared adventure with the God who so longs for us to be the women He designed us to be: women who are confident in His love; who follow His Son for their purpose in life; who are empowered by the Holy Spirit and who look beyond their small corner to a wider waiting, hurting, world.

We so often forget that we each have just one life. We waste it daily, minute by minute, when we fail to live in the *true confidence* God has for us. We squander the gifts He has given *every* one of us when we fail to recognise, let alone use, those gifts.

We are greatly loved by God, so loved that He gave His all for us. Yet so often we live a 'half-baked' life, as if we have been given nothing – and have little to give. We need God-given confidence. Confidence that does not depend on success, popularity or shoulder pads, but which is built on nothing more than what God says about us: a confidence that has everything to do with Him and little to do with us; a confidence that leads us away from 'me' and into a passion for 'them' – the wider world God aches to have know Him.

If that's the kind of confidence you long for, read on …

Chapter 1

True confidence is …
not what you think!

'But blessed is the man who trusts in the Lord, whose confidence is in him. He will be like a tree planted by the water that sends out its roots by the stream.'
Jeremiah 17:7–8

I t was a hilarious idea: in fact it still is. The idea of *ME* writing a book, writing anything, in fact, about confidence: it is hardly the first characteristic on any list I might compile about myself. In fact, I doubt whether confidence would make it on to the list at all. It is something I have struggled with all my life.

I have a vivid memory of myself, aged ten, two long fair plaits hanging over my shoulders. I am standing at the front of the class. Chalk dust from the blackboard behind my head is tickling my nose and the room is swirling before me: a sea of classmates' faces. I have been asked to read my story to the class – again. For some reason, today, for the first time, I'm feeling a lack of the quiet confidence I normally find in the story I've written and in the joy of sharing it. Instead, despite the encouragement of my teacher, I am terrified.

Even now, more than thirty-five years later, I can remember the names and faces of the 'popular' children who sat before me then, with what I believed were the first twitches of mocking amusement tugging at the corners of their mouths. What could the quiet, arty bookworm with the straggly plaits possibly have to offer them? That day must have contained the moment when self-consciousness crept in, as it inevitably does for most of us. The moment when we begin to compare ourselves with others and notice that, in our eyes at least, we do not quite match up.

I became a gawky adolescent wallflower who turned into an often inappropriately loud teenager. To be loud, flirty and giggly hid my shaky self-confidence. As those 'lively' years ebbed away into 'grown-up' student life, I lost the hiding place that being loud and lively gave me. At parties I found that a better tactic was to sink into the background and spend as much time as possible in the kitchen.

And so on into my adult life, when really I should have been old enough to know, and be, better. Two incidents stand out amongst the parade of 'Where was my confidence?' scenarios. The first involved my participation – or rather non-participation – in an exciting and innovative creative development meeting at which I had much to offer but throughout which I was totally overawed by the other personalities present. Many were 'head' of this or 'in leadership of' the other. They spoke louder than me, put their ideas forward faster and drew the acclaim and approval of their contemporaries gathered around the table. What could I have to offer alongside them? At the end of the meeting I recognised that I had failed to share ideas that would have been equally valid and creative (perhaps more so) and which might have helped the whole team to produce an even better plan. I left the event feeling that I had let down God, myself and the team, yet again. Such was my distress that on the train home afterwards I silently wept behind my sunglasses, filled with gnawing inadequacy and failure, and scolded myself for yet another missed opportunity to share my gifts. I had probably appeared aloof – lacking in the skills and experience needed and as if I had nothing to offer. Those present probably wondered why on earth I had been asked to attend. Lack of confidence had ambushed my life once again. I did not expect to be asked to develop my role in the group – and I never was: that fact continues to cause me pain and heartache.

The second incident was a more recent one. Just three years ago, at a large national Christian event, I was asked to lead mainstream teaching seminars with a friend who is (if we should make such estimations) one of the most popular and respected Christian speakers and leaders in the UK. He is loved, applauded – and sometimes criticised. But his speaking gifts, his integrity, his achievements and his credibility are second to few. To say that I felt like a feeble sidekick bathed only in his glory is an understatement. After all, everyone had come to hear *him* speak: most wouldn't even know my name. I was just there to fill the gap.

He noticed – as he would. 'You're very good at this, you know,' he said at the end of the first seminar. I beamed and said thank you, and then came the characteristic, honest punch: 'So why don't you believe in yourself, then?'

I was stunned. Just by sitting behind me as I spoke and watching me as I worked he had spotted my lack of confidence and my sense of inadequacy – however 'good' I had been.

In the months since the conversation that followed I have replayed those words so often. Yet I know – as I have been reminded writing this book – that God has confidence in me. It is why He stands me up in front of hundreds of people and asks me to speak or gives me a passion and asks me to write about it. It is why He trusts me with projects like this one. (And why CWR does too!)

Yet, at the very heart of what I do, I am sometimes strangled by self-doubt and fear, often underperforming simply because I'm lacking in self-confidence.

But there's the rub, I think. Because it isn't *self*-confidence, confidence in myself that I need, that any of us need; not exactly. What we need is confidence once-removed: confidence in the confidence our Father places in us. Confidence in the Person of Jesus, His Son, as our role model and confidence in the Person of the Holy Spirit as our guide, our comforter, our inspiration and our source of empowerment.

I have realised, slowly, that when I display a lack of self-confidence, I am actually showing a lack of God-confidence: a lack of trust. Because I am essentially saying: 'I don't believe that I can do this'; 'I deny that You have given me these gifts'; 'I cannot accept that You have made me this way for a purpose'. I recognise, too, that all those words – spoken or unspoken – must hurt my Father God, who has given me so much to use for Him – but also simply for my own joy and delight.

I share my experience and my thoughts, not because I want you to feel sorry for me (or to wonder why on earth I wrote this book!), but because I want you to know that I have not 'got it all together'. I have not 'arrived' where confidence is concerned. I do not swan around daily in a posh business suit, networking at speed and adding international contacts to the ever-growing address list in my glossy little black book. I am not fighting off dinner invitations from an ever-widening social circle. Rather, I often wonder why the phone doesn't ring; why I wasn't asked to do this or that; or whether I 'blew it' at that talk or meeting as much as I thought I did.

I am still on a learning curve. Sometimes I get stuck on it, my feet rooting me to the spot in numb terror – sometimes I fall off it altogether! There are days when I shock myself with how confident I can feel, act and be and I wonder who this person is to whom other people are responding so well. And then I realise it's me! What's more, it's the 'me' that God made me to be. Sometimes there's no explaining why that happens. On other days, I'm bereft of anything resembling confidence. My heart aches as I recognise those old familiar feelings of self-doubt, waving their equally-familiar discouraging scripts round and round in my head – and I feel like reaching for my sunglasses behind which I can cry.

I know that I need a different confidence: 'God-confidence'. A confidence that reassures me daily that God is 'for me'. A confidence that doesn't slip away on bad days or evaporate in the face of the giftedness, criticism or expectation of others. A confidence that comes from more than just knowing my stuff, rehearsing well, being within my comfort zone or wearing the suit that makes me feel as if I could run the country.

I am beginning to understand what 'God-confidence' – *true confidence* – is, but I still have a long way to go before I find myself truly living within it.

I am on a journey. I hope that you will join me on that journey through the pages of this book, as we recognise that God is for us and that we can live the life He designed for us in the *true confidence* He gives.

A model of confidence:
the Elle Macpherson factor!

Firstly, let's deal with a few myths.

Most of us live our lives woefully overshadowed by what I call the 'Elle Macpherson factor'. Now, for those of you happily ignorant of the name, Elle Macpherson is a so-called supermodel. She, apparently, has it all: grace, beauty, money, superstardom – and even her own lingerie company. So beautiful and flawless is she that she is known as 'The Body'.

Now I know that owning a lingerie company – or having 'The Body' – are not what we all aspire to! But, whether we admit it or not, most of us do aspire to the kind of level of success – the level of confidence – that models and celebrities like Elle Macpherson demonstrate. We may have our own local version of Elle Macpherson (even if she or he is not a supermodel) working alongside us, living near to us, or as part of our church family. He or she makes us feel, probably quite unintentionally, about two centimetres tall.

We look around us and, on the bad days at least, everyone else seems to have all the confidence we should have – and more. We sneak a look at them with something resembling envy, and mutter, 'Why can't I be like her?'; 'I will never be like that …'; 'I'm not like her …' Well, exactly. There's only room for one Elle Macpherson, supermodel, in the world. In fact, there's only room for one Wendy Bray, struggling writer and 'growing-in-confidence-although-you'd-never-know-it' speaker, too.

There is only one of every single 'one' of us. It is not God's way to make us identical in gifting or looks (unless we are an identical twin). Each of us is unique and that's the way He wants it. If not, why did He make so many variations of individual you and me? Why do we not daily come face to face with at least seven of our own doubles?

Women like Elle Macpherson may or may not be our role models. But they are not supermodels of confidence. They don't serve us well: in fact they sell us short. We know God doesn't wants us to be 'like them' – but like us. Finding *true confidence* is not about becoming 'like them', whoever 'they' are. It's about becoming as much 'like me' in all my uniqueness, as God intended. It's about becoming fully and wholly the person He designed me to be. Not a sidekick of a bigger name, but the apple of God's eye; reflecting *His* glory, not somebody else's. The only model for that kind of confidence is Jesus. He is a very different kind of supermodel!

In our celebrity-led world, we have turned confidence into something cosmetic: a characteristic dependent on style, talent, ability or success. But Jesus models humility, not fame; confidence in His Father, not in the flimsy accolades of reputation, wealth, magazines and media campaigns.

There's nothing wrong with having a role model: someone we admire and whose approach to life we strive to emulate. Indeed, it can be helpful to learn from the success of someone else – or even to ask them to coach or mentor us. But we need to choose wisely. We need to choose someone closer to us than the TV screen or magazine page: someone who is more likely to be a realistic model of confidence.

The first thing we need to do as we embark on this journey is to dismiss the empty assumptions that popular, disposable culture attaches to confidence. We need to begin by examining what confidence really is: to identify its source and discover how we can begin to see it flowing into our lives.

What *is* confidence anyway?

The dictionary defines confidence as: (1) 'a consciousness of one's powers being sufficient …'; (2) 'faith or trust in something or somebody' *The New Penguin English Dictionary.*[1]

In essence, Christian confidence rejects (1) for the guaranteed security of (2). It rejects the temporary confidence-boosters of style, talent, ability or success. It doesn't depend on any of those fleeting things. *True confidence* is far from fleeting: it is eternal.

True confidence is, essentially, trust. Not trust in a particular business strategy; not confidence in our own ability, or even in that of a team member or strong and reliable friend or partner. Instead, Jeremiah tells us, 'But blessed is the man who trusts in the LORD, whose confidence is in him' (Jer. 17:7). Jeremiah paints a picture of a tree that draws its sustenance from a river: its roots spread out to draw up the water offered, ensuring that it never becomes dry. Instead the tree grows strong – heavenward – and stands firm. Times of drought or heat may come, but the tree remains well watered and strongly rooted to the spot – and never fails to bear fruit (Jer. 17:8).

Interestingly – and appropriately – the NIV Study Bible states that the same Hebrew root word (*bitachon*) underlies both words, 'trust' and 'confidence'. In this passage from Jeremiah that root word extends to include the source of a righteous man's (or woman's) strength: a strength that is like the very roots of a tree itself, not planted, but *trans*planted to a safe and well-watered place.

When we ask God to take charge of the direction of our lives, He does, literally, transplant us from a dry, arid, self-controlled (and often weedy!) plot to one that is well watered, with Him as a source of life. Of course, that doesn't mean we will avoid times of drought or exposure to too much heat – they are still mentioned by Jeremiah. Desert times are a familiar and important part of faith. Rather, we need not fear when 'heat' comes or worry when life appears to have 'dried up', because the faithfulness of God, the gift of Hhis Son and the power of the Holy Spirit are an ever-flowing source of sustenance.

They don't dry up on bad days or divert themselves to the man or woman of the moment. Instead, the source of confidence given by God is timeless, yet eternal; not transitory but constant; not fleeting but lifelong and life-focused.

The confidence God offers is confidence for life.

True confidence is … for life

For some of us, knowing God means that we are just now embarking on what is a new and exciting relationship. For others, it has been a long-term, even lifelong partnership. We are able to say that we have known God 'since [our] youth' (see Psa. 71:5–18).

What we sometimes forget, amidst either experience, is that God has always longed for us and craved relationship with us. We were His hope, long before we knew He was ours. That's hard to grasp, isn't it? Especially if we have been battered by difficult relationships or carry a low sense of self-worth. It's hard to understand that the God of the universe should seek relationship with us at all, let alone take the initiative! But He loved us *first*, and sometimes He chases us across the years until He catches us in an embrace to whisper, 'I have always loved you.' But if we can understand that longing of God's, that chase, that embrace, even just a little, how could we not find confidence in such love?

I know a young couple whose lives were transformed by the confidence their love for each other has given them both. James was quiet and shy, withdrawn – almost nobody could reach him. Then he found himself working alongside Jayne: bubbly, warm and accepting, but scarred from a difficult childhood. She found in James the stability and thoughtful seriousness she needed. James found a bright personality who drew him from the shadows to show him that life – and love – were worth the risk.

Jayne knew security for the first time, while James came out of his hiding place and into the light. They fell in love. Those present at their wedding say that it was one of the most joyous they had ever been part of. It was a public declaration of a private confidence. Today, Jayne and James both say that they feel they had unknowingly been waiting for each other. They have grown into their marriage in a confidence that is rooted in love – giving each other hope. Finding each other has transformed their lives.

God's love can transform us even more than that. His love is not limited like human love; it is an everlasting love with an eternal hope.

Sometimes, because of our own experiences, it is difficult for us to allow God to reach us and draw us from the shadows into His light. It may take an enormous step of faith to draw nearer to God. We fear intimacy because we fear the pain of loss or have experienced too much disappointment or betrayal in our human relationships. Some of us may need to take a deep breath or a great leap of faith before we can allow God to catch and embrace us. In a sense, we need to 'unlearn' the lessons forced upon us by our earlier experiences in order to understand that God's love is not subject to human limitations, weaknesses and frailties. God's very nature is love and that love provides us with a firm foundation for our confidence.

True confidence is ... based on a foundation of love

Child psychologists tell us that to become a fully-rounded and confident individual a child needs to know and, more importantly, experience something of the three 'S's: Self-worth, Security and Significance.

It is not enough for a child just to be told: 'You are good. You are safe. You are valued.' Those messages have to be communicated in actions and priorities as well as words, and as part of a loving relationship: a relationship based on unconditional love – love without strings.

God is many things to us: King, Creator, Saviour and Lord – each inspiring a different kind of confidence. But He is first and foremost our Father. In the parent–child relationship we can have with God those very elements – self-worth, security and significance – are demonstrated in the most amazing ways. Very significantly, God demonstrated their essence by giving His Son to save us in the ultimate act of unconditional love.

Secondly, the Bible underlines each of them constantly. Let's look closer at some scriptures that remind us of that.

Firstly, *self-worth*. Genesis 1:26 reads, 'Then God said, "Let us make man in our image, in our likeness ..."'

Being made in God's image – the Imago Dei – means we have intrinsic worth and dignity. It is, if you like, a worth that has been carved into our very being by the hand of God. When He created us as human beings He saw something 'very good'

(Gen. 1:31). We are modelled on Him and He made us. Who are we to quibble with His design or His assessment?

Secondly, *significance*. In 1 John 3:16 we read, 'This is how we know what love is: Jesus Christ laid down his life for us.' And the Gospel of John: 'For God so loved the world that he gave his one and only Son ...' (John 3:16). So significant are we, so loved, that Jesus gave His life for us as individuals and for the whole world. Look at the names and numbers of the references of those two verses. It always sends a tingle up my spine to see that these two significant statements that proclaim God's sacrificial love for both the world and the individual are so very similar in name and number; one in a Gospel, one in a letter: we *matter* to God! He wants to tell us – loud and clear!

Thirdly, *security*. Proverbs 29:25 reads '... whoever trusts in the LORD is kept safe'. Whatever happens to us we are safe in God's protection – although not necessarily in physical terms. Faith does not give us immunity from accidents, disease, tragedy or loss. But it does give us much more – eternal security. Jesus says, 'I give them eternal life, and they shall never perish; no-one can snatch them out of my hand' (John 10:28).

But it's not just isolated verses like these that remind us of the foundation of our self-worth, significance and security, and therefore our confidence – although it is worth remembering these words on a daily basis.

Rather, the whole of God's love story with us, as shared in the Bible, is one of chasing and wooing, protecting and delivering, forgiving and loving, heading for a fabulous finale: a homecoming. Yet it is a story not without pain and suffering, anguish, betrayal, jealousy or anger. God is a gracious God but He is also a God of justice. The two must go together.

Our foundation for confidence is built on His omnipotence as well as His mercy. But ultimately we know from the relationship history that God has with His people – and very probably from the history of our own individual relationship with God – that it really is true that there is nothing we can do to make God love us more and nothing we can do to make Him love us less. His love is constant, solid and unchangeable. It holds us firm, safe and close. In that relationship we have a perfect foundation in which to know confidence. For, as Paul says, 'If God is for us, who can be against us?' (Rom. 8:31).

Ask yourself

• Who do I consider to be my confidence 'role model' and why?

- In the light of what I have read is he/she a helpful and encouraging model? Or does he/she need replacing with a 'new model'?

• Do I have issues with significance, self-worth and security that have damaged my view of the foundation of unconditional love God offers me?

- Might I need to talk those issues through prayerfully with a wise friend or counsellor?

• Do I really believe God's estimation of me – that I was made in His image and am loved 'so much' that He gave His life for me?

- What can I do to make that knowledge – and that
  message – part of my daily life and motivation?

For reflection
. . . .

Think back through your life and your relationship with
God. Chart it on a timeline with paper and pen, if you find it
helpful. Where do you notice evidence of His unconditional
love or gracious guidance: reminders that 'there is nothing
you can do to make God love you more and nothing you can
do to make Him love you less'? What does this mean to you?
How might it influence your view of yourself?

You may find it helpful to complete this exercise together
prayerfully with a partner or friend who knows you well.

Prayer
*Father God, remind me that I am Your child: valued, chosen, safe.
Release me from self-doubt; from the inadequacies caused by the
failure and disappointment of the past, and enable me to stand
before You as You see me – as a loved and precious child. May
Your love for me become the foundation of my confidence. Amen.*

1. *The New Penguin English Dictionary* (London: Penguin
   Books Ltd, 2000).

Chapter 2

True confidence is … based on the unchanging nature of the Father

'For you have been my hope, O Sovereign LORD,
my confidence since my youth.
From my birth I have relied on you …'
Psalm 71:5–6

Confidence in the God who is constant

Life today is changing at a faster pace than ever before. We battle to master some new aspect of technology, only to do so days before the next advance is announced – making our skills, once more, inadequate. Leadership roles and political allegiances move from one person or party to the next before we can even remember the names of the politicians or pinpoint their policies. And fashion? Well, fashion changes with such speed that it goes full circle! I find myself looking at styles my mother wore when I was twelve!

Most of us have learned to live with change in a fast-paced world, but in order to do so we need some constants in our lives – particularly within our relationships.

Children face a number of major life changes – like starting, and changing, school. They adapt to these with much greater confidence if they do so from within the security of a loving family setting which models strong relationships. They need a safe and stable 'springboard' from which to launch into their new lives: a springboard that has a large and cosy sofa at the end on which Mum, Dad or Gran is perched and to which they can retreat whenever necessary.

In terms of needing security and stability in our relationships, nothing much changes as we grow into adulthood. Knowing that we are loved builds our self-esteem; knowing that such love is constant and reliable gives us security – not just in the relationship offering us that love, but also in all our forays into the outside world as we seek to build new relationships. Sadly, not all of them will be quite as reliable.

Like me, you have undoubtedly heard someone say, 'I never know where I am with him' or, 'She is always changing her mind'. An ever-changing, irresolute character is hard to deal with. We remain unsure, despite assurances. Experience teaches us to doubt and never quite believe the word given – however earnest the promise.

Some of us may have known such uncertainty in parental or marital relationships. We may have grown up or grown into a life where much is unpredictable and few things are constant. It can be hard to grasp the concept of the Fatherhood of God if our own father has been less than faithful or loving; if he was often absent or unreliable, always changing his mind and his plans.

But God's nature, be it as Father, Creator, King or Lord, is to be constant – both in love and intent. He is ever present and ever reliable: His plans cannot be thwarted, as the Bible documents so clearly. Psalm 33:11 tells us: 'But the plans of the LORD stand firm for ever, the purposes of his heart through all generations.'

The beautiful psalm from which this verse is taken has the stability of God's character written between the lines for us to read. It speaks of righteousness, truth, faithfulness and security, reminding us that God made the world in which we live. It reminds us that He has filled it with His love and that He holds firm to His plans for it, foiling the schemes of wayward nations and pushing forward His greater eternal purposes. It is a psalm that clearly illustrates His unchanging and constant nature. In simple terms, He made us, He holds us and He will keep us: period.

Whatever our TV screens and newspapers might tell us, God is in control, it is His world and He holds our future. He remains quite unfazed by the headlines and straplines we produce. They may sadden Him – even break His heart – but He is above and beyond every word, remaining powerful and ever present within and through the world events they communicate.

When my children were small, my daughter (two years and nine months older than her brother) would often lend him her beloved wooden tricycle. She always made it clear that even though he might be driving it (on loan), it still belonged to her. Every so often, even as he was sitting on it, she would grasp the handlebar and steer it in the direction in which she wanted it to go. It's a crude and simple illustration, perhaps, but God has His eye on where He wants His people 'to go'. His plans remain unchanged. However often we appear to veer off His path, He will steer us – and His world – towards the fulfilment of His constant purposes. We always know where we are with God. Our names are ever before Him: engraved, permanently, on 'the palms of [His] hands' (Isa. 49:16).

Our confidence for the future need not lie in the decisions of men; rather it is better placed in the constancy of God, as we trust the purposes of His heart.

Confidence in the God who is loving

Earlier, we observed that God remains powerful and ever present within and through world events. But His presence isn't always easy to spot, let alone to believe in. Questions assault us with their demand for an answer: Where was God for the majority of those involved in the Boxing Day Tsunami? Where is He in the death of that young child in our village? In the handicap of disability? In the ravage of cancer or the terror of rape? In the face of such questions our confidence can often waver. At first we want to find answers, but we fear the glib and unhelpful Christian platitudes so often given to the suffering by those who have little experience of their situation. We cringe when scriptures are flung into a place of pain without practical care and consideration for those sitting in that place. It's tenderness, not teaching, that the vulnerable

27

need from us. But, often, we don't know how to offer it or what it should contain.

What we do know is that God is not absent from our suffering: in Jesus He was 'a man of sorrows, and familiar with suffering' (Isa. 53:3).

When I was facing months of arduous cancer treatment, I found great comfort in Jesus' Gethsemane experience. Not because the treatment I was about to face was anything like the agony He would suffer, but because I knew that He understood how I felt in facing pain, uncertainty and bewilderment – even as I trusted in the Father. His prayers became my prayers. I found Him in His dark place and He came into mine.

I have spoken to others who will say with certainty that, despite the pain, grief or terrible difficulty they were facing, they did find something of God in the darkest of places. That doesn't mean that they never felt alone; that they never felt as if they'd reached the end of their resources; that they didn't cry out to God in anguish or anger. Just that there was something like a pinprick of light in the darkness – a pinprick of the light of faith giving them a sense of God's love, in spite of their suffering. Somehow, God becomes bigger than the suffering itself. He stands in front of it and blocks the view with His love, even if He does inevitably move aside once more, leaving us to its pain. Somehow we can cope better because we have seen what really matters: God, the God whose love will bring us through, 'whatever'. And what's more, our promised salvation will bring us, ultimately, to Him.

The apostle Paul knew something of that love and hope in a place of suffering. In his second letter to Timothy, he writes, '... I am suffering ... Yet I am ... convinced that he is able to guard what I have entrusted to him for that day' (2 Tim. 1:12). What an inspiration Paul's letter must have been to Timothy!

Despite the probability that Paul was under house arrest at best, and in a cold, dark cell at worst, he still held fast to his confidence because it was based on more than comfort or circumstances. He remained sharply and even joyously aware of the salvation he'd been given and the promise made by the Lord Jesus, stating confidently: '... I know whom I have believed ...' (2 Tim. 1:12). His confidence was placed in the certain knowledge that the Saviour would 'deliver' as He had promised.

Paul encouraged Timothy to guard the gospel and keep the faith until 'that day' through the love of the Lord Jesus Christ and the power of the Spirit.

His confidence was a 'whatever' confidence.

'Whatever' has been adopted by teenagers as rather a throwaway word, implying indifference, a passive agreement or a 'don't care' attitude. Surely it is miles away from Paul's use of the word here? Well, yes – and no. Paul was in some sense 'indifferent' to his suffering (although not in an adolescent way) because it was taking him closer to his Lord. He was in agreement with what was happening to him because he knew that his pain and discomfort were nothing compared to an eternity in God's presence. He really *did* say, 'I don't care', about his circumstances. Because he knew they were only that: circumstances.

God was, in effect, 'standing in front' of Paul's suffering and blocking the view. Paul's 'whatever' wasn't a negative, throwaway word, but a positive and certain word of confidence. A word of faith – 'whatever' his circumstances.

We so often let our faith drown in our circumstances. A little bit of discomfort and inconvenience, insecurity or uncertainty has us whining to God with a 'Why?' and a 'Not fair'. We lose sight of the bigger picture, allow our confidence to be shaken and forget that, 'whatever' happens, God is in control.

Perhaps we should ask a teenager to help us learn to say 'whatever' with a shrug of the shoulders. It might become a word of faith!

Confidence in a God whose love watches over me

When my daughter Lois (the aforementioned owner of the wooden tricycle) was very small, she was somewhat fearless when it came to playground equipment, clambering up the climbing frame like a monkey and balancing on the very top rung to wave to me. She would fling herself from the top of the slide like her namesake, Lois Lane – as if daring Superman to rescue her. It was hard to keep her safe without harming her confidence: many a prayer was muttered by this anxious mother as Lois clambered high above the hard ground!

Her brother was, by contrast, a much more timid soul. Whether he recognised her recklessness or just preferred to stay closer to the ground, I'm not sure. But he was much more wary of climbing and needed my reassurance. We faced something of a struggle regarding his confidence in me when he began to utter the phrase: 'Mummy, watch me, so that I won't fall.' Not, 'Watch me, in case I do fall' – so that you can pick me up and kiss me better – but 'Watch me, so that I won't'. Wouldn't that be a wonderful ability for a mother to have? Yet I had to teach my son that although I was there and would watch him, I couldn't guarantee that he wouldn't fall. Rather, he would need to rely on his own judgment and experience – and a little bit of faith – to stay above the ground, rather than landing on it prematurely. I would be there to help and guide, to encourage and applaud, and even to mop up tears and wipe knees if all went wrong, but I didn't have any ability to ensure his safety.

For most parents, it's not the fear of accidents happening when we are watching over our children that concerns us the most. It's what happens when we are separated. Those two children are now adults living away from home at university. That clambering six-year-old girl is now a confident twenty-one-year-old, who will not climb anything unless it leads to a dress shop, restaurant or bar. That 'little boy' is now 6 foot 4 inches tall and enjoys climbing up the mini-mountain, Arthur's Seat, behind his university residence in Edinburgh!

I am now separated from both of them; their safety cannot be my responsibility. Once again, they are asked to rely on their own judgment and experience and that little bit of faith. And in that faith I pray for them daily. I also remind myself that even though they are separated from me and (although I hardly dare imagine) whatever happens to them, nothing can separate them from God's love.

In his letter to the Romans, Paul tells us that he is 'convinced' of that fact. He doesn't just hope that it is the case or think so on a good day, he is *convinced*. Convinced by his own judgment, by his experience and by his faith:

> Who shall separate us from the love of Christ? Shall trouble or hardship or persecution or famine or nakedness or danger or sword? ... No, in all these things we are more than conquerors through him who loved us. For I am convinced that neither death nor life, neither angels nor demons, neither the present nor the future, nor any powers, neither height nor depth, nor anything else in all creation, will be able to separate us from the love of God that is in Christ Jesus our Lord.
>
> Romans 8:35,37–39

In his book, *Love Beyond Reason*,[1] writer John Ortberg tells the story of a bear cub who becomes separated from his father in a snowstorm. Lost in the blizzard, the cub comes face to face with a wolf that has had his eye on the youngster for some time. Believing himself isolated and vulnerable, the cub can only do what he has seen his father do when faced with an enemy: rear up on his hind legs and growl. But when the little bear does so, his hind legs wobble and his growl is a mere squeak. He is not convinced – neither is his predator. The outlook is not good. Just as hope is almost lost, the terrified cub watches in amazement as the wolf cowers, turns and runs away, snarling. He then realises that behind his own weak attempts his Father has appeared out of the storm. He has also risen to his more powerful height and growled like thunder to protect his son. The cub feared that he had been separated, but his father, keeping him in view, stepped in at the last to save him.

We often feel as if we're separated from God by circumstances: fear, illness, redundancy, loneliness – all that Paul mentions and more. But our God is Lord of all – even of what threatens us. Paul reminds us again that our circumstances will not separate us from God. He sees everything. He watches over us. He will sometimes keep His distance in silence or remind us of our dependence on Him as we wait, even until we believe He is lost, and often until we are hanging on by a thread. But His grace-filled love keeps us in sight, no matter how fierce the storm or the enemy. He will always rise up behind us at just the right moment.

His protection may not always be physical, immediate or what we would ideally want. Often we won't see Him, hear Him or be aware of His presence – but He is there. Even the fear of the future and the pain of the past do not separate us (v.38). There are no circumstances that can create a gulf between us and our Father God. Nothing, absolutely nothing, separates us from His love: we are inseparable.

Confidence in a God who saves me from myself

Actor Stephen Fry is also a brilliant writer, conversationalist and comic. Feted by fellow actors for his wit, his words and also his compassion, he has spoken bravely and helpfully about his own experience of manic depression. He explains that when he is in the depths of despair he blames himself for his predicament, telling himself that life is going wrong because he is useless and worthless. His self-degradation is so venomous that he refers to himself with an aggressive torrent of names – most of which would be unrepeatable in polite company. He says that the torrent is almost a Tourette's syndrome of self-condemnation.

Many of us are quick to condemn ourselves – if not in the face of mental illness, in the face of our own weakness. We constantly play back our failures and moments of falling; we beat ourselves over the head with their most 'magnificent' moments and wish we could undo the damage. In so doing, we often condemn ourselves to hours, days, years (and, in some cases, a lifetime) of carrying guilt and remorse.

It's inevitable that our failure and weakness will impact our confidence, not just before others or before our own mirror, but before God. 'After all,' we reason, 'who am I, after all I have done? Because of all I am as a person? How can I stand in confidence anywhere, before anyone, let alone before God?'

We may imagine a business meeting between us and our image of God: we enter a large and empty boardroom. Everyone else has left, of course, because they have done their job well. Their items and actions were approved in the meeting and have been ticked off the 'To do' list. But we have blown it again and there is the chairman, God, seated at the far end of the shiny boardroom table. He taps His pen on His clipboard and we wait for Him to read the minutes of the meeting we have missed and to find out what 'matters arising' refer to us and our sinful state. And we wait for the dressing down that must surely come.

But Paul, once more writing to the Romans, says that condemnation isn't even on God's agenda for us if we know Jesus and are in relationship with Him. In effect, that boardroom scene is simply a figment of our imagination. It's a meeting that doesn't happen. It's been cancelled. Cancelled out by God's love for us: 'Therefore, there is now no condemnation for those who are in Christ Jesus' (Rom. 8:1).

As a child, my friends and I would pass an almost derelict property on the way home from school. We would dare one another to open the rusty gate and run up the garden path or to pick up fallen apples from the grass beneath the apple tree. We called it the 'Old Witch's House' and it terrified us!

Some years later, older, wiser and with a little more compassion and understanding, I discovered that an elderly woman had lived there alone. Her neighbours had offered to repair and renovate the house but she had rejected their offers of help, often unkindly, until they had given up. Years went by. In spite of the fact that the house had been condemned and she had been offered alternative accommodation, she stubbornly refused to move. Eventually, she died in the squalor from which the Social Services had tried to save her. Having chosen to live in a state of 'condemnation', she had died in it too.

It seems nonsensical to us for someone to pass up comfort and care to remain in squalor and loneliness. But often we are no different. Some of us choose to live in the self-condemned property that is our life. Even when offered a brand-new life, free, purpose-built and secure, we prefer to live surrounded by the rubble of a life that we ourselves have condemned – with guilt or regret. We allow our actions, our choices and our circumstances to condemn us to low self-esteem, failing confidence, anger and depression.

We may struggle to build anything again or blankly refuse because it takes too much effort. Neither will we move away from the debris and the ever-present dialogue of depression that does so much damage. We prefer to live in our comfortably self-condemned life, listening, as Stephen Fry does, to the Tourette's syndrome of self-abuse.

But that's not the dwelling place God has chosen for us.

God's dwelling place for us is not one of condemnation but of grace: grace in partnership with repentance and a desire to live His way. If we live God's way 'in Christ Jesus' there will be no condemnation for us – now or in eternity.

If God doesn't condemn us, why do we condemn ourselves? Why do we listen to those negative words and believe the names we call ourselves? It is His grace that justifies our very existence, His love that chose us and set us apart, so why do we allow circumstances, self-criticism or the painfully-remembered words of others to condemn us?

Sometimes we just need to choose to live somewhere else. Yes, it may be stressful initially – moving often is! But we need to recognise the condemned state in which we're living and work to do something about it. That might mean praying through our self-assessment and self-condemnation with a wise friend, asking for forgiveness and letting go of guilt. It might also mean letting go of the 'furniture' of our lives that has kept us sitting in comfortable condemnation. It might also mean avoiding the roads that lead us to its door: the habits, memories, props – even the people, who direct us away from

God's view of ourselves and, importantly, from the life He has planned for us. It's only when we move out of our condemned lives that we will discover how to live in the confidence and grace that comes from the assurance of God's love: '… there is now no condemnation …' (Rom. 8:1).

Where will you choose to live?

Confidence in a God who believes in us

When completing magazine quizzes we often face A–D multiple choice questions or lines of boxes into which we must tick our 'Yes' or 'No' – and even our 'Maybe' – answers. With choices A–D, it's often easy to work out which box we have to tick to come out on top, so that we can close the magazine with some self-satisfaction. Quizzes where the answers are 'Yes', 'No' and 'Maybe' require a little more honesty on our part. It isn't often that we are able to answer a complete set of questions in the affirmative – and even then our affirmative 'Yes' answers may be designed to indicate that we are indeed as 'challenged' at communication, confidence or casserole cooking as we always believed we were! The positive answers can end up making us feel negative!

But that's not the case with a God who believes in us. He ticks all our 'Yes' boxes. Firstly, He loves us so much that He has given His all for us. He believes in us! Ultimately, His opinion of us is the only one that matters. We can be safe, secure and confident in His assessment of us: 'If God is for us, who can be against us?' (Rom. 8:31).

Secondly, all that God has promised since the beginning of time is fulfilled in Jesus. Jesus Himself gives those promises their 'Yes'. He underlines them, emphasising the constancy and faithfulness of God, the security of the message He brings and the Person He is.

In his second letter to the Corinthians, Paul reminds his readers (and us) that the message of Jesus has been found to be entirely true: '... in him it has always been 'Yes'. For no matter how many promises God has made, they are 'Yes' in Christ' (2 Cor. 1:19–20a).

Paul explains that Jesus is the fulfilment of all the promises His Father has ever made. He claims us as His own and guarantees what is to come. There is no doubt, no wavering, no 'Maybe' between the 'No' and 'Yes' answers – just affirmation in the Person and love of Jesus. Those guarantees should impact every area of our lives – not least our prayer lives.

When we pray the kind of prayers that God would have us pray – those that line up with His love and His longing for us – it is through Jesus that our 'Amens' can be spoken with confidence. 'Amen' means: 'It is true' or 'So be it'. It is a positive, God-confident statement at the end of our prayer or praise. Yet so often we mumble it into our collars or our cleavages! We need to change our habits: say 'Amen!' with assurance and to God's glory. It is the 'Yes!' of faith; a great big 'Yes!' of salvation and joy.

My son is generally a relatively quiet individual. He takes life pretty much in his stride and keeps most of his feelings to himself. But just occasionally he allows himself an extravagance of emotion. If a goal is scored or he gets the results he wants (on passing his driving test, for example) he leaps around a bit, punches the air and yells 'Yes!' It's more than a celebration of fact – it seems to me like a celebration of life!

I often wonder if we should sometimes adopt that exuberant action at the end of some of our prayers, especially prayers of praise and thanksgiving. Just think of Jesus, punch the air and shout 'Yes!' If Jesus is the great affirmation of all God has done for us, surely we shouldn't be mumbling the fact into our collars – but proclaiming it with confidence!

So, answer 'Yes' or' No': can you be confident in the unchanging nature of God's love?

'Yes!'

Go on … punch the air!

Ask yourself

- Have I experienced the constant nature of God's love?

  - How does it contrast with the nature of the human love I have known?

  - What might I learn from that?

- Has my faith been shown to be 'whatever' faith?

  - How did God make Himself known to me in that 'whatever' place?

- Do I have a tendency to remain in a place of self-condemnation?

  - What do I need to do to move out?

  - Do I want to?

For reflection
••

Look at yourself in a mirror.

Why do (most of us) find it hard to do so?

What does God see when He looks at you – according to what you have learned in this chapter?

Write a few words to remind yourself of how God sees you and how you are held in His constant love. Place those words above the mirror.

Prayer

Father God, when You look at me You look at me with the greatest love I will ever know. Teach me to be confident in the unchanging and constant nature of Your love. Remind me that there is nowhere I can go and nothing I can go through that can separate me from that amazing love. Amen.

1. John Ortberg, *Love Beyond Reason* (Grand Rapids: Zondervan, 1998).

Chapter 3

True confidence is … modelled on Jesus

'Your attitude should be the same as that of Christ Jesus …'
Philippians 2:5

So who *IS* your role model? We talked light-heartedly earlier about the 'Elle Macpherson factor' – and how, so often, we choose role models whose lives are unrealistic for us to base our own upon; people who really aren't such good role models after all. It isn't usually very long before we recognise our poor choices, witness their 'fall from grace' and are glad that we can't be like them, after all.

With Jesus, it's a very different scenario. We know that He is the best role model for living we could possibly have; that He lived a perfect human life and wants us to follow the way He lived. But although we know He is a perfect and reliable role model, we seriously doubt our ability to live as He lived. He may have been human – but He is also God. How can we possibly match up? After all, we're hardly the 'perfect man' or 'perfect woman'. Does that mean, then, that Jesus is also, for very different reasons, an unrealistic role model? Well, yes – and no.

Of course it's unrealistic for us to 'match up' to Jesus. But that doesn't mean He can't be an excellent role model. It may not be a perfect allegory, but imagine a young schoolgirl just embarking on a promising running career. Marathons are her life and winning the New York marathon is her goal: Paula Radcliffe is her heroine. Should she reject the Olympic champion as a role model because she fears she will never 'match up'? No, of course not. Instead, she keeps Paula Radcliffe at the forefront of her mind as she trains: the lifestyle, training schedule and motivational sayings of her role model become the motivation and inspiration for a young champion-in-training.

What we have to remember, of course, is that although Jesus is Teacher, Master, Leader and role model, He is also something that no Olympic champion could ever be: the chosen and anointed Son of God. That makes Him far more than just a champion to emulate. Although God does anoint us for special tasks and ministry (as we'll discover later), Jesus' anointing is special and unique. But that doesn't mean He can't be our role model for a life of faith.

Looking at the life He lived, the words He spoke, the ministry He was called to and the priorities He lived by, offers us a blueprint for life. They teach us how we can grow in confidence, as we allow Him to be our role model as well as our Saviour.

Learning from Jesus, the Anointed One

Jesus' ministry began with His Father's anointing. His confidence came from the fact that He was specially commissioned for the task: 'The Spirit of the Lord is on me, because he has anointed me to preach good news to the poor' (Luke 4:18). Jesus spoke these words in the synagogue before a gathering of His contemporaries. Whether He chose to read these beautiful words from Isaiah or whether they happened to be among those already selected for this particular day, we don't know. Either way, they were fulfilled before the very eyes of everyone present. He proclaimed a very special blessing of God: not the anointing of oil that those listening would have been accustomed to, but the anointing of the Holy Spirit.

Anointing with oil was both an everyday celebratory practice for bestowing honour (perhaps for a guest) and a sacred one. Sacred anointing was a practice begun with Moses under God's direction (see Exod. 30:22–31). It was first used for the anointing of Aaron and his sons as priests and for marking the tent of meeting and its contents. Even the fragrance and purity of the oil were given great attention by God: He specified the ingredients as well as the use.

The anointing of Jesus, however, was unique. It indicated

both honour and fulfilment. This anointing with the Holy Spirit showed that He is the Messiah (which means 'anointed one') and that, as Old Testament prophecy indicates, He fulfils the roles of prophet, priest and king, each of whom were anointed by God.

It's true that God still 'anoints' us with honour today and often does so with His Holy Spirit, offering us guidance and strength to face special tasks or responsibility. This may be done in the context of prayer alongside others, often with the laying on of hands or the anointing of oil, as we ask for God's help and wisdom. It is another way for God to equip us with the confidence we need to serve Him. If we know that God is calling us to do something specific for Him – to train for ministry, perhaps, or to develop a special gift in our church family – His anointing can seal our response to that calling, giving us the commissioning and the confidence we need to step out boldly to do His work, as He has sent us.

For Jesus, this anointing with the Holy Spirit marked the beginning of a confident, bold and Spirit-filled teaching and healing ministry: a life in which He did the work of His Father who sent Him.

If Jesus the Son needed the anointing of the Spirit for His work, how much more do we?

Learning from Jesus as He lived

As well as being an anointed Son, Jesus is also a chosen Son – and Servant: 'Here is my servant whom I have chosen, the one I love, in whom I delight ...' (Matt. 12:18). Once again, the words of Isaiah are used to proclaim Jesus in fulfilment of Old Testament prophecy: this time as the chosen Servant King (Isa. 42:1–4). These words would have been familiar to onlookers on this occasion, onlookers who doubtless gossiped among themselves, speculating about who Jesus was and what His mission was to be. So much so, that Jesus had to warn them not to tell others. Jesus was, and is, that past hope fulfilled as well as our promised hope for the future. His earthly life was spent offering that eternal hope to all who would listen and respond.

But, of course, He offered that hope in a unique and wonderful way. He didn't force His way into lives with an arrogant swagger, wielding a manifesto for the privileged. Neither did He take His place at the head of an accompanying army, as many of His contemporaries had hoped: God's way is not our way. Instead, He became His Father's servant – and also the servant of those He came to save.

Servanthood: it's not exactly held up by contemporary role models as the route to confidence, is it? *Hello* magazine does not include features on 'Celebrity Servanthood' does it? But servanthood was certainly a part of Jesus' confident ministry – so it should be a part of ours.

If we look closer at these words and their context we can see the qualities that mark out His servanthood. Jesus offered hope and salvation with authority, gentleness, respect, dignity, grace and mercy – as well as with a lot of very practical common sense! The Servant King offered His kingdom by serving others in order to bring them into the very palace courtyards He had left behind. No wonder this man was unique!

We are 'chosen' by God to live our lives in just the same way – as servant children of the Servant King, with the help, counsel and enabling power of the Holy Spirit. Servanthood is both the source and a symbol of *true confidence*.

We have already seen how the ministry of Jesus (as prophesied by Isaiah) and its practical outworking (as recorded by Matthew) illustrate some of the hallmarks of Jesus' life.

He showed authority, gentleness, respect, dignity, grace and mercy. We can learn much from those qualities as we develop confidence in our own personal 'servant ministry'. They turn the popular view of 'a confident person' on its head. According to Jesus' model of confidence, 'a confident person' is not loud, successful, good looking and assertive (or the life and soul of the party), but is respectful, dignified, gracious, merciful and imbued with gentle authority: the complete opposite, in fact! That makes developing confidence a whole lot easier, doesn't it? Especially with Jesus as our role model.

Learning from Jesus as He worked

Those hallmarks of Jesus' ministry – gentleness, respect, dignity, grace and mercy – reflect what mattered most to Him as He worked. As He did His Father's will in introducing the kingdom, Jesus had just two priorities: people and prayer.

With those priorities and despite the fact we are told that He 'had no beauty or majesty to attract us to him' (Isa. 53:2). Jesus *must* have been an engaging personality. Those pressing crowds we read about in the Gospels tell us that He was someone who everyone wanted to be with.

You may have noticed that the people we like being with most are those who take interest in us, who focus on our concerns and needs and who genuinely seem to care about our wellbeing. People who show genuine interest in us make us feel special.

Jesus' genuine interest was based on compassion and an urgent desire to save the lost by reuniting them with His Father. He often asked searching questions and sometimes gave a direct challenge. But, far from presenting His concern in doom and gloom or by piling on the 'evangelistic' pressure, Jesus shared that desire and compassion in the context of genuine, authentic relationship. He also did so with joy and with perfect confidence in His Father: 'At that time Jesus, full of joy through the Holy Spirit, said, 'I praise you, Father, Lord of heaven and earth …' (Luke 10:21).

I wonder what it was about Jesus on that particular day that made Luke write that He was 'full of joy through the Holy Spirit'? What made that joy obvious to onlookers? Something in His manner or in His beaming smile? It's certainly something I would love to have said about me! What better compliment could we be given? Certainly beats 'You look nice' or even 'I admire your confidence'.

It was Jesus' confidence (in His Father) that gave Him such joy – there's the irony. And He shared this joy not only with His Father, in this amazing prayer recorded by Luke, but also with His followers.

The 'seventy-two' had just returned from their first preaching and healing mission full of joy (v.17) to tell Jesus excitedly of the wonderful things done in His name. We can almost imagine them falling over themselves with gushings of 'And *then* …' and 'You'll never guess what …' Of course Jesus didn't have to guess – He knew. Nevertheless, He catches their excitement and praises His Father for the consequences and meaning of their experience. They had been engaged in the work of the kingdom of God – and they were buzzing!

Those followers – the first New Testament ambassadors of God's love – must have been somewhat sceptical when they set out on that first mission. The instructions Jesus had given them were clear enough, but they were hardly prepared and their apparent resources were few. Nevertheless, God used them, resourcing them with the power and confidence that only the Holy Spirit gives, working through them and sending them back amazed and full of excitement. God chose to reveal 'these things' to them (v.21); to involve them in His wider mission because of their willingness – cautious and sceptical or not – to go out in His name.

In the same way, we can serve Him in obedience to His 'sending out'. Even when we feel less than prepared, we have His resources and His blessing. And we'll return 'with joy' when we go where He sends us to work for Him, trusting in His resources rather than in our own, and living and working in the confidence He gives us through the Holy Spirit. More about that – and the Holy Spirit – later! Because, as we'll see, the Holy Spirit still wants to reveal the amazing 'things' of the Father to us, just as He did to these excited early followers of Jesus. The spiritual resources and blessing He gives are another source of *true confidence*.

Learning from Jesus as He speaks

If Jesus' approach to those He met was gracious and respectful, His words undeniably had impact: '"No-one ever spoke the way this man does," the guards declared' (John 7:46). The content and message of Jesus' words, as well as their delivery, drew people to Him – and we forget sometimes just how far people would have walked to hear Jesus speak!

People listened to Jesus. What He said mattered to them. His words may have shocked, challenged and rebuked those He addressed at times, but His listeners hung onto and quoted His words widely, both one to another and further afield. They had never heard anything – or anybody – like Him.

Yet Jesus wasn't just some kind of moral teacher, neither was He just an entertaining conversationalist or storyteller. His message melted hearts, met needs and changed lives, and it did so whilst all the time He blended those two priorities of people and prayer.

How we use words is such an important part of a life lived confidently. What can we learn from the way Jesus spoke?

Firstly, Jesus related to people 'where they were at'. He didn't expect a special audience or arrange extraordinary meetings – although those meetings often became extraordinary! Rather, He met a wide variety of people in their day-to-day activities and busyness. He took an interest in them and often used elements of their work as an illustration for life and faith.

Some time ago I wrote an article for *Christianity* magazine about supermarket chaplains – church leaders who, often voluntarily, spend time in their local supermarket chatting to and supporting both staff and shoppers. Some of them have become a more familiar sight in the aisles where shelves are piled high with baked beans than in the aisles of their church building! They have recognised that the supermarket is both a place of work and a place of life. They know that the supermarket is often where people spend a good amount of their week: especially the lonely elderly, for whom the supermarket is a source of company and activity in an often empty day. People are on familiar territory in a supermarket: they are often more relaxed and more able to talk about their lives and their problems in a familiar everyday setting. Conversations that begin with 'What are you going to cook for tea tonight?' often lead to something that is far more profound or heart-searching than simply discussing how many sausages are needed! Some of the chaplains have been asked to baptise babies, marry customers or staff (to each other!) and, often, to hold worship services at Easter, Christmas and Harvest – inside the store. They understand the importance of speaking to people 'where they are at', of valuing the routine of their daily lives and work and of recognising that God is present in the detail.

Secondly, Jesus spoke to people in different ways: as a coach or mentor, as an encourager and as a teacher – but always as Lord.

Jesus doesn't appear to have taught formally. Instead He told stories, using metaphor, simile and allegory to give His words visual presence in the minds of the people He spoke to, building pictures they could relate to and remember (Matt. 7:24–29). He wasn't all theory and no practice either. He interacted with His 'pupils' and modelled the 'How to do it' part of the lesson before their eyes in His everyday life. His teaching was active, 'hands on' as we would say, and His disciples shadowed Him, learning alongside Him on the job like apprentices (see Matt. 12:1–13). Jesus expected the people who listened to Him to hear and act – especially those chosen disciples.

He taught large groups on hillsides and mentored small groups as He walked; and He often engaged individuals in intimate one-to-one conversation about their own lives (Luke 18:18–30). And, like every good coach, Jesus asked lots of questions, drawing people out and making them think.

Thirdly, He had a clear goal. Everything Jesus taught focused on a new way of living: life in God's kingdom. With that goal in place He never missed an opportunity to draw people to His Father. He used His surroundings, agriculture, custom and humour, I believe, to reach those goals and He never let His listeners lose sight of 'the main thing'. It made His words and their message surprising, challenging, often puzzling, but always compelling. But Jesus was pragmatic in His use of words, too. It's easy to think that He only ever said things that were very worthy or in sermon form. But I'm sure He spent a lot of time talking about the weather, just like the rest of us! And we know that He spoke about where His next meal was coming from and where He might rest. Jesus' words were practical as well as prophetic. He addressed people's physical needs as well as their spiritual longings. That, in itself, teaches us something valuable about how we should talk to people, as we seek to share our lives and our faith.

Jesus was often tender, always straightforward, frequently painfully direct and never afraid to engage people both in serious debate (Luke 10:38–42; 14:1–14) and in rambling (probably often light-hearted) conversation.

I think that we disregard the importance and potential of our conversation. It's as if familiarity breeds contempt. 'How can God possibly use idle chitchat over a cup of morning coffee?' we say. But, in my experience, He uses that 'chitchat' more than He uses powerful oratory from a pulpit. It's often in chance conversation and passing words that God speaks most powerfully. If we have the confidence to listen to His promptings and make the most of the opportunities He gives us He will let our words speak in ways we can only marvel at, even if we don't realise their impact at the time.

I once met an acquaintance for coffee (I'll call her Sue) to offer my support.

A mutual friend (whom I'll call Sarah) had recognised our shared experience of cancer and felt that Sue might benefit from my 'been there, done that' wisdom. She did not share the faith that Sarah and I shared however and, although I was wary of being too full of 'God-talk', I knew that I could not separate my experience of cancer from my experience of God within it. I didn't want to miss any opportunities to share God with Sue, but neither did I want to get it wrong. So I simply prayed: 'Be in that conversation, Lord. Give me opportunities to say the right thing.' So Sue and I met in a lovely riverside pub where we talked about family and chemotherapy and laughed at wig stories and, well, God didn't really seem to come up at all, except in passing. At the end of our time together I felt that I hadn't done much to help and neither had I shared my faith. Feeling a complete failure, and scolding myself for not being bolder, I arrived home feeling rather sad.

That evening, my friend Sarah phoned. She told me that Sue had just called her to ask to go to church with Sarah the following Sunday – if that was OK. 'What *DID* you say?' Sarah asked. 'I've been inviting Sue to church for years and she always says no!' I was as lost for clues as my friend – but was delighted. Later we discovered that I had said nothing specific that had attracted Sue. Rather, reading between my lines, she'd discovered something of my confidence in God's ability to hold my life in His hand, not in a grim and threatening way, but in the joy of a relationship between Father and daughter. Sue's own relationship with her father had been close and special. She had seen parallels, which meant that, unknown to me, she had been intrigued. I, meanwhile, was flabbergasted. In committing that conversation to God I had allowed Him to work – His way. I thought that I had wasted my words – but God hadn't. He had worked wonderfully within my limitations.

Jesus never wasted a word: His words were life-giving. God may just give us words that are life-giving too, often at the moment we least expect them.

Learning from Jesus as He suffers and dies

As Jesus' time on earth came to an end He knew that He'd almost completed the 'work' for which He had been anointed. As the final act of sacrifice and love was about to take place, He prayed one of the most beautiful prayers recorded – for Himself and for His disciples (John 17:1–26). This prayer illustrates the perfect confidence Jesus has in His Father. Confidence both in the day-to-day work He had been given to do (now almost finished) and in the way in which His Father would complete and bring to fulfilment all that He had begun.

But His prayer and His confidence were not without real human struggle. The account of His time in Gethsemane (Luke 22:39–46) gives us a glimpse of Jesus, the human God, in the face of fear and anguish. Yes, He had confidence in His Father, but that didn't mean He did not struggle with what He was being asked to do.

These final prayers are a profile of Jesus' very real conversation with His Father: a model of honesty, weakness, submission and trust. If Jesus is our model in His life, work and teaching, He is our model here, at the end of His life, in the very face of suffering and pain: '"Father, if you are willing, take this cup from me; yet not my will, but yours be done." An angel from heaven appeared to him and strengthened him. And being in anguish, he prayed more earnestly, and his sweat was like drops of blood falling to the ground' (Luke 22:42–44).

Notice that Jesus' anguish did not end with the strengthening of the angel. It continued. What mattered was that He was strengthened in the midst of that pain and suffering. The anguish and fear were not taken away; rather God met Him in the very midst of them.

When I was undergoing a stem cell transplant for cancer some years ago, I knew something of this godly intervention in suffering. It was the early hours of the morning and I was horribly weak from intensive chemotherapy, hardly able to shuffle from my bed to the adjoining bathroom just a few feet away in my tiny isolation room. But with a desperate need to reach the loo, as the chemicals repeatedly upset my stomach, I contemplated how on earth I would make it – for what seemed the millionth time that long night. So, I decided to carry my pillow and take up residence in the bathroom, sleeping as I sat! With the edge of my pillow clenched between my teeth, I shuffled across the room, two intravenous drip stands (complete with drips) my only support. I reached the loo and slumped down. Suddenly, I felt worse than I'd ever felt before. Moving in and out of consciousness, I realised that my weakness was defeating me: I was going to faint – or worse. Oddly, my sense of humour kicked in even then, as I thought, 'I cannot die on the loo – I will never live it down!' The thought that I wouldn't be around to 'live it down' did not occur to me!

But, in that dreadful weakness, I remembered – a thought from 'nowhere' – that there is power in the name of Jesus. I repeatedly whispered His name with my remaining strength. Suddenly, I felt held from behind. Two hands, under my armpits, lifted me out of the weakness for just a few minutes. At first I thought it was a nurse. But the wall filled the narrow space behind me – no one could have stood there. Too weak to care, I was able to rest in a wonderful Presence that upheld me for a short while until I was able to open my eyes and eventually regain the strength to shuffle back to my bed. I enjoyed the best night's sleep for weeks and, as I slept, I dreamt. In my dreams I was being wrapped in large white sashes that bore words of love and encouragement: 'precious', 'beautiful', 'loved'. I was held close and secure – and being reminded as I slept that it could only have been God who, in some way, had reached down into the very heart of my weakness and been in it with me.

In our Gethsemane moments, be they of weakness, terror, despair or anger, the Gethsemane experience of Jesus shows us that it is OK to fear. It is also OK to be honest with God. It's OK to feel weakened and desolate – and OK to question all we are asked to do for our Father – because of our relationship with God and our faith (confidence) in Him. That confidence may only have the strength of a flickering match threatened by a wind of unbelief. However, as long as it is lit we can know confidence – even in the darkest hours of our lives.

Remember: sometimes it's as if God stands in front of our suffering, just for a moment, before moving reluctantly aside once more. He reminds us that He is bigger than all that befalls us.

At the very last, Jesus turned to His Father in a final act of trust and abandonment: '"Father, into your hands I commit my spirit." When he had said this he breathed his last' (Luke 23:46).

God is our confidence in life and our confidence in death.

Ask yourself

- Do I too easily reject the notion of Jesus as 'the human God' and so fail to learn from Him as a real human role model?

- Which aspects of that 'modelling' do I find most challenging? His attitude to work? To prayer? To speech? To relationships?

- Which elements of Jesus' confidence in His Father might I transplant to my own life – starting from today?

For reflection

Have you known times when God has stood in front of your suffering, assuring you of His love? Remind yourself of these times. As you do so, acknowledge the pain and the, as yet, unanswered questions and reaffirm your trust in His love for you.

Before moving on to Chapter Four, spend time looking at some of the questions Jesus asks in the Gospels. Read them as if He were asking *you* the same questions.

You might look at some or all of the following: Matthew 6:25–34; 7:7–10; 9:27–30a; 14:31; 16:8–11; 18:1–4; Luke 6:46–49; 7:36–50; 8:40–48; 9:20; John 4:4–26; 5:1–9.

Write down your responses.

How might those questions and answers build your confidence in Him?

Prayer

Jesus, Yours was the perfect life of true confidence: *a life built on confidence in Your Father. Help me to remember that He is my Father, too, and that my true and complete confidence can also be in Him. As I reflect further on Your life show me how I might learn practical confidence from Your priorities and Your purpose. Amen.*

Chapter 4

True confidence is … maintained and empowered by the Holy Spirit

*'Now the Lord is the Spirit,
and where the Spirit of the Lord is,
there is freedom.'*
2 Corinthians 3:17

Confidence that is founded on the Father and modelled on the Son needs maintenance and empowerment. And that's where – and why – the Holy Spirit comes in.

The NIV Thematic Study Bible tells us that the Holy Spirit is: 'the co-equal and co-eternal spirit of the Father and the Son, who inspired Scripture and brings new life to the people of God.'[1] It also tells us that the Holy Spirit: 'equips and empowers believers so that the reign and reality of God is revealed through them in the world.'

Those words explain both the *Person* and the *purpose* of the Holy Spirit. It follows, then, that when we live lives that are open to Him, the Holy Spirit comforts, inspires, convicts, guides, counsels and empowers us. In doing so He gives us confidence in our faith and for our future.

The Person of the Holy Spirit

The Holy Spirit's mission and purpose is a uniquely personal one. He is 'the up close and personal' God, sent to remind us of Jesus' teaching and promises, and to enable and empower us to live by them: 'But the Counsellor, the Holy Spirit, whom the Father will send in my name, will teach you all things and will remind you of everything I have said to you' (John 14:26).

Sometimes, sadly, we have poignant conversations with those we love, knowing that they will be our last together. Something in the finality of the situation prompts us to make the most of those moments. Jesus was similarly prompted to 'make the most' of these last conversations with His disciples (John 14). Having taught them all He is able, He knows that they still have so much to learn. So He promises them that His Father will send Someone who will continue to teach them and remind them of all He has already shared with them – the Person of the Holy Spirit.

Too often, we think of the Holy Spirit as a nebulous 'thing'. We understand the concept of God's power displayed through the Spirit, but the *Person* of the Holy Spirit is more difficult. Yet the language used of the Holy Spirit is always personal language because He is a divine *Person*. It is He who gives new life, liberating us and enabling us to believe. He makes us God's children, equips us, inspires us, opens our eyes to God's Word, shows us more of the Father and helps us to pray. Yet He will never overwhelm us in a way that we cannot cope with. Instead He will make us more and more what and who we were meant to be: He offers us the way to *true confidence*. In fact, He is a little like a spiritual life coach!

These words of Jesus from John's Gospel clearly introduce the 'Personhood' of the Holy Spirit. He is described as Someone of truth and constancy who will live with us – and in us. We may find that idea puzzling, but as we get to know the Holy Spirit more as a *Person* we realise that a loving Father and a Son, given to serve and save mankind, could not leave us to live in the world without the third Person of Their Being living close for our company and comfort. He is so close to us that He actually lives within us and around us. Shouldn't that unique closeness and security inspire a special confidence?

The promise of the Holy Spirit

The Holy Spirit is with us in fulfilment of a promise: Jesus said, 'Do not leave Jerusalem, but wait for the gift my Father promised ...' (Acts 1:4). That promise – and that Person – is known best when our relationship with the Spirit is built on *faith* and *expectation* as well as *action*.

When my son was small, he liked to know what the day might bring. He needed some forewarning and security in the shape of promises and assurance, for example: 'We will go to nursery this morning and to the Post Office sometime after lunch and, yes, you can definitely buy your chocolate buttons then.' But he also had to learn that much would have to be taken on trust: 'I don't know exactly when we will go yet – but we will go.' Jesus obviously sensed that the disciples, in their anticipation of losing Him, needed similar assurance (although, perhaps not about chocolate buttons!). They also needed to learn to trust Him in His absence. So He gave them specific directions as to what they should do – and a broader picture of hope. He grounded those instructions and assurances in both the unshakeable promises of His Father and in the everyday experience of remembered conversation: conversation they had shared. In effect, He told them: 'this is what you must do', 'this is what you can depend on' and 'this is what you already know'. For the rest they had to trust Him. Their confidence was built from three angles: knowledge, faith and action. When we need confidence to do what God is asking of us we can do the same: know what we believe, have faith in His promises – and get on with the job in hand!

The Holy Spirit also fulfils another promise. It's the promise of a broader picture of hope – the promise of eternal life: 'Having believed, you were marked in him with a seal, the promised Holy Spirit, who is a deposit guaranteeing our inheritance until the redemption of those who are God's possession – to the praise of his glory' (Eph. 1:13b–14). 'Guarantee' and 'deposit' sound rather businesslike, don't they? We may even be fazed by such words, wondering whether they are really worth their meaning. Despite their grand sentiment, they may leave us feeling not altogether secure. Guarantees are rarely watertight in our cynical litigious world. They often come with exemptions, opt-out clauses and small print, even when they are supposed to be safeguarding our position. Deposits should, technically, secure a purchase or place for us. However, we can never be really certain of their value until what we had hoped for has been received and paid for in full. Until then, our hope isn't secure.

But when God the Father gives the guarantee, our hope is based on 'the word of truth' and marked by the Holy Spirit – so we can be confident. We don't even have to 'pay the bill'. Jesus paid the price in full. The presence of the Holy Spirit in our lives is a lifelong reminder of the completeness of that 'transaction'.

Too often we live our Christian lives unable to grasp that fact. We can't quite accept that everything is signed, sealed and to be delivered later. It might help to remember that we are already living in God's kingdom in this life – we've just got the best part of our inheritance to look forward to. Meanwhile, the Holy Spirit, our guarantee, can be the source of our confidence in that certain outcome. He will remain with us until our hope is fulfilled.

These words of assurance from Ephesians help us to fully appreciate how the Father, Son and Holy Spirit work together to give us this wonderful guarantee. There is no hidden small print, the price is paid in full, and our hope *is* secure.

The comfort of the Holy Spirit

Jesus promised that the Holy Spirit would come to teach, remind and counsel – but also to comfort and reassure. It is His comfort that we are able to pass on to others in empathy:

> Praise be to the God and Father of our Lord Jesus Christ, the Father of compassion and the God of all comfort, who comforts us in all our troubles, so that we can comfort those in any trouble with the comfort we ourselves have received from God.
>
> 2 Corinthians 1:3–4

Sometimes the comfort given by the Holy Spirit is unexpected, even inexplicable: a sense of peace in the midst of tragedy or turmoil; a sense of company in times of loneliness; a reassurance that all will be well, when it would be easy for us to believe anything but.

One of my friends tells the story of driving across country in order to reach her mother, who was dying. Devon to Scotland is a long journey at the best of times – but when you're anxious to arrive in time and are concerned about the isolation and pain of those you love, a car can be a very lonely place indeed.

My friend left home at about 5am, as soon as her father called. Within just a few hours, the traffic had built up for the morning rush hour and then crawled for miles because of a collision. Becoming increasingly distressed, my friend felt her tiredness and emotions running together into a pool of despair. Through her tears of impatience and anxiety, she begged God to ease the traffic jams, remove the juggernauts, give her car wings ... 'Anything, Lord, just get me there!'

But God did not move the juggernauts or send her soaring skyward in the direction of Inverness. Instead, she felt prompted to drive off the motorway and found herself almost immediately in a small village where she parked her car, deciding to take a walk. She found the church and, in the churchyard, a bench where she decided to sit for a few moments in the gentle morning sunshine. There she felt the unexpected and overwhelming comfort of the Holy Spirit and knew clear reassurance that she would arrive at her mother's bedside 'in time': she only had to drive. Calling into the village shop for something to eat and drink, she mentioned her journey to the shopkeeper who kindly made her a cup of tea and a piece of toast. As she chatted, she relaxed further, reassured by both the comfort of God and the care of a new friend. She arrived in Scotland at supper time and was able to spend precious time with her mother who, although unconscious, seemed aware of her presence and died peacefully just a few hours later.

Not all of us will 'get there in time' in such circumstances. But we may know the comfort and reassurance of the Holy Spirit who understands and who was sent specifically to comfort and counsel us (often very practically) at such difficult times. The Holy Spirit may often be practical and proactive in His leading and comfort, as He was with my friend, but He also enables us to pray – and when we can't, He prays for us: '… the Spirit helps us in our weakness. We do not know what we ought to pray for, but the Spirit himself intercedes for us …' (Rom. 8:26).

I am rarely lost for words in conversation (!) but I am often lost for words in prayer. Sometimes words cannot express the depths of our pain – or our joy.

At other times we know we can do nothing *but* pray – we just don't know *what* to pray. It's then that the Holy Spirit, living with us, will communicate for us. When we turn to Him, expressing (even wordlessly) the depth of our emotions or the complexities of our situation, He will catch them up in a prayer (audible or otherwise) that communicates in a way our inadequate words just can't.

I have often prayed simply through my tears. Overwhelmed with grief, pain, helplessness or frustration and unable to form any words, I have just wept my prayer to my Father God. Jesus knew this kind of sorrow (Matt. 26:38) and the Holy Spirit '… intercedes for us with groans that words cannot express' (Rom. 8:26).

I mentioned earlier how, when cancer treatment had weakened me and I felt at the very edge of my life, I remembered that there is power in the name of Jesus. As I whispered His name in the darkness the Holy Spirit carried my plea and 'filled in the gaps' of my prayer. He intervened for me – from, in and through the depths of my weakness.

We don't have to find the words to pray – we just have to find the faith. Even faith weakened by sorrow or almost driven away by pain can be transformed by the Holy Spirit into the prayer we need to pray. When we are 'lost for words' the Holy Spirit finds those words and carries them in prayer on our behalf, giving us confidence that we are heard.

The guidance of the Holy Spirit

The Holy Spirit is also a source of confidence as our Counsellor and Guide.

I mentioned earlier that in some ways He is like a 'spiritual life coach'. But He is unlike a life coach in that He is able to change our thinking as well as our choices and priorities: 'The mind of sinful man is death, but the mind controlled by the Spirit is life and peace' (Rom. 8:6). He works in partnership with us to transform our thinking and give us confidence in a right way of living.

In his letter to the Romans Paul explains, in his typically uncompromising style, that our new lifestyle demands a new mindset: one controlled by the Holy Spirit. We baulk rather at the idea of 'mind control'. It smacks of hypnotism, loss of freedom – even dictatorship. Yet if the Person of the Holy Spirit is really living within us and we are 'born of ... the Spirit ...' (John 3:5–6) who brought us into a relationship with the Father, we will *want* Him to 'dictate'. He will not do that by seizing control, robbing us of choice and running off with our intellect, imagination and free will. Instead, He stands with us – even within us – to guide, help, inspire, empower, embolden, counsel, comfort, teach, love and sometimes rebuke. We just have to learn to listen to Him and so learn more of His mindset and the way in which it can shape our own.

No one is saying that's easy to do. We all have minds that wander, thoughts that shame us and imaginations that don't always entertain the dreams and desires they should. Thank goodness our minds aren't transparent! But, of course, they are to God. And for that reason we can be honest with Him and ask Him to strengthen that special 'mindset' partnership with the Spirit. As we do so, we can have confidence that, if we are earnestly looking to live God's way, we will know the comfort and 'coaching' of the Holy Spirit.

The inspiration and gifts of the Holy Spirit

It would be easy to think, from our considerations so far, that life with the Holy Spirit is about sitting in a peaceful place, feeling comforted, or making sure that He is guiding our frequently errant thoughts. But, thankfully – and excitingly – there is so much more to Him than that!

You may remember that our definition of the Holy Spirit's character and work said that He 'equips and empowers believers so that the reign and reality of God is revealed through them in the world'. The exciting thing is that the Holy Spirit enables us to be part of God's mission in the world; we are 'one of the team'. What's more He doesn't just encourage and comfort us or pray with us as we work in the team: He actually gives us the gifts we need to do the job! In other words, through the Holy Spirit, God says, 'Don't just sit there! Do something!'

As a student, I was involved in a challenge in which six of us, using our resources and skills, had to find some way to cross a river (for example, by building a bridge or raft). There were severe restrictions on our resources and we had to do it by pure improvisation. Scuttling off in our search to find the means, it was frustrating to have to pass punts, rowing boats, floating piers, kayaks and paddles. We just weren't allowed to use them to cross that green and wet expanse: we had to use new initiative and method. Needless to say, there was much high-speed driving, bargaining, pleading and floundering around at the edge of the river. We got very wet and muddy in the process – but we made it eventually. We also learnt that paddling pools were not made to cross rivers!

So I am relieved that God does not leave us entirely to find our own resources – especially in a church 'team'. Instead, through the Holy Spirit, He gives us specific skills and abilities to use for the benefit of the team:

It was he who gave some to be apostles, some to be prophets, some to be evangelists, and some to be pastors and teachers, to prepare God's people for works of service, so that the body of Christ may be built up ...

Ephesians 4:11–12

More specifically,

Now to each one the manifestation of the Spirit is given for the common good. To one there is given through the Spirit the message of wisdom, to another the message of knowledge by means of the same Spirit, to another faith by the same Spirit, to another gifts of healing by that one Spirit, to another miraculous powers, to another prophecy, to another distinguishing between spirits, to another speaking in different kinds of tongues, and to still another the interpretation of tongues. All these are the work of one and the same Spirit, and he gives them to each one, just as he determines.

1 Corinthians 12:7–11

We have to remember that these gifts are just that – gifts. We are not entitled to them and they are not to be boasted of, used inappropriately or kept to ourselves. They are, Paul says, 'for the common good'. Everything that God the Father knows we will need to live lives of love, trust, obedience and service within and from our Christian communities is provided by these gifts.

God equips, enables and empowers us to do all He asks us to do for Him as we love and honour each other, by the power of His Holy Spirit. If we sincerely look to Him for spiritual resources to build our confidence, we will not flounder around helplessly or sink. We need only ask.

The power of the Holy Spirit

The Holy Spirit gives those gifts in power, of course. But He also gives them quietly and usually without fanfare, 'so that the reign and reality of God is revealed through them in the world'[2]. The power of the Spirit has been demonstrated throughout history. It is power that was witnessed in creation (Gen. 1: 2); through the life and witness of His servants (Micah 3:8; 1 Sam. 10:6; Isa. 63:11–12); in the life and ministry of Jesus (Matt. 7:28–29; Mark 1:22–27); as well as in the Church's mission to the present day.

The Holy Spirit's power and intervention is frequently prayed for but is often unexpected. Like electricity that operates a light bulb but also powers a lightning strike, the power of the Holy Spirit can be specifically and quietly channelled but also powerfully unpredictable – enabling the Holy Spirit to show both His tenderness and His boldness.

In the early chapters of Acts we watch amazed as He transforms a group of shaky, nervous men into powerful preachers – especially in the case of Peter, whose very human story of transformation we will look at later. Jesus had said,

'But you will receive power when the Holy Spirit comes on you; and you will be my witnesses ...' (Acts 1:8). Paul also declared that his words were not his own but from the Spirit:

> I came to you in weakness and fear, and with much trembling. My message and my preaching were not with wise and persuasive words, but with a demonstration of the Spirit's power, so that your faith might not rest on men's wisdom, but on God's power.
>
> 1 Corinthians 2:3–5

Those words have reassured many a reluctant sermon-giver, including me!

I remember very clearly the day I gave my first sermon in my home church. I'd done a considerable amount of teaching up to that point, in seminars and meetings for Care for the Family for whom I worked at the time, but I didn't enjoy it at all. I really didn't think it was my gifting or calling. What's more, I'd never preached from God's Word directly to a congregation. But I was asked to begin an Advent sermon series which was based on my Advent book, *The Art of Waiting*. The subject was Martha and Mary waiting for Jesus to arrive to raise their brother Lazarus from the dead. This account had impacted me powerfully and personally in my own spiritual journey – but sharing it with 400 others in my home church was quite another matter. To say I was reluctant is an understatement.

In the weeks beforehand I cried, fought and pleaded with God. How could I preach on such a powerful story? Who was I to stand in that pulpit? Where would I find the words? God patiently (and with some amusement, I believe) reminded me that the words were already written in the book He had helped me to write; that the insight into the story He had already given me was enough. I did not have to rely on myself, but on the Holy Spirit. He encouraged me to read the story of Peter's first sermon once more and to meditate on Paul's words to the Corinthians, mentioned above (1 Cor. 2:3–5), assuring me that I would know the Holy Spirit's presence and power.

Finally, the Sunday morning I'd dreaded for so long arrived. Fearful, apprehensive and so nervous that I hadn't been able to eat breakfast, I climbed the steps into the pulpit. In the few moments before I began I could only quietly mutter, 'Here goes – over to You, Holy Spirit.' And then, something extraordinary happened. As I began to unpack that wonderful story of Jesus' love, compassion and intervention I was carried along by joy and enthusiasm. I was able to express my passion for the account – and I loved every moment of sharing it.

At the end of the service, as my feet hit the carpet at the bottom of the pulpit steps, I had the distinct impression that God was saying to me: 'Well done, good and faithful servant!' I knew a clear and wonderful sense of His joy and delight. In my weakness and fear the Holy Spirit had truly empowered me. This marked the beginning of a new phase of speaking and preaching. It was very different to what had gone before because, like Paul and Peter, I had forgotten my own lack of self-belief and had spoken in the power and confidence of the Spirit.

The often unpredictable and very personal power of the Holy Spirit was not confined to the New Testament Church. He carries on God's mission and ministry in our lives and worshipping communities today (Acts 2:17–18) – and not just by giving words to reluctant preachers! Against all odds He turns hearts to God; He heals both physically and emotionally; He pours the peace of reconciliation into the bitterness of estrangement; He gives words of wisdom where the words of men are not enough; and He enables churches to bring the grace, love and mercy of God to their communities, in ways both practical and miraculous.

In all these ways the power of the Holy Spirit amazes us – bringing us to thankfulness and worship. The glory is God's alone. But in all this He also gives us confidence in God's way of living and confidence in our hope for the future: 'And hope does not disappoint us, because God has poured out his love into our hearts by the Holy Spirit, whom he has given us' (Rom. 5:5). That confidence is not placed in men or method, but in an all-knowing, all-present, all-loving, all-powerful God, who longs to be part of the lives of His people – if only they would ask: '... let us draw near to God with a sincere heart in full assurance of faith ... Let us hold unswervingly to the hope we profess, for he who promised is faithful' (Heb. 10:22–23).

Ask yourself
- How well do I know the Holy Spirit?

- How much do I ask – and allow – the Holy Spirit to lead, guide and inspire me on a daily, hour-by-hour basis?

- What might He be asking me to do that will move me out of my comfort zone – but into a place of His empowerment?

- Regarding my spiritual gifts – is there a wise Christian friend I can ask to pray with me about discovering them and their use?

- Have I known specific times when I have been given the confidence – or comfort – of the Holy Spirit? When, and how, might I be assured of both?

For reflection

Read Galatians 5:16–25.

What practical advice about maintaining a life of confidence in the Holy Spirit does Paul give here? Which words challenge you most?

Write out verse 25 and keep it somewhere visible to remind you daily of its encouragement: 'Since we live by the Spirit, let us keep in step with the Spirit.'

Prayer

Holy Spirit, I long for You to be such a part of my life that my confidence is maintained by Your inspiration, guidance and comfort. Help me to meet Your Person daily and to be open to Your power, hour by hour, and minute by minute. Amen.

1. *The NIV Thematic Study Bible* (London: Hodder and Stoughton, 1996) pp.1415–6.
2. Ibid., p.1416.

Chapter 5

True confidence is … not about me

'Then, leaving her water jar, the woman went back to the town and said to the people, "Come, see a man who told me everything I ever did. Could this be the Christ?"'
John 4:28–29

When my daughter Lois was just entering those awkward early-teenage years she struggled with self-consciousness and a lack of self-confidence. On one occasion Lois said that she wished she could walk around concealed by a large brick wall! As this arrangement wasn't too practical, there had to be another way to help her realise two things: 1) that she was beautiful, inside and out – that understanding might only come with love and time – and 2) that the very act of being self-conscious could only have a detrimental effect on her lack of confidence.

Over the course of several months, she began to understand that people who are self-conscious actually draw attention to themselves – simply because they look so ill at ease. I demonstrated this fact one morning, as we sat in a coffee bar watching a succession of girls walk past in the shopping mall. She realised, as I did, that the most attractive and confident-looking were rarely those who would be considered the most physically beautiful. The most 'beautiful', in reality, were those who walked easily, with heads held high, but not too high; those whose smile seemed about to break across their faces; or who looked approachable, interested in other people and as if they were enjoying or were positively challenged by everything life might offer. Some of the most conventionally 'beautiful' (who should, by popular assessment, have been the most confident) appeared to carry their beauty as a burden. They peered around suspiciously, to see whether anyone had noticed that their make-up wasn't quite perfect or that they'd eaten two slices of toast for breakfast instead of a bowl of low-calorie cereal.

Of course, what my daughter really needed to know was that much of her awkwardness would disappear if she forgot herself and concentrated on others. As she learned to know, understand and love her emerging womanhood, in relationship with others, a new confidence would establish itself: the surrounding wall would not be needed.

At twenty-one she is now a confident young woman who has learned those lessons well. We often remember those shopping-mall coffee-bar days and knowingly remark to one another how much more lovely 'so and so' would be if only she could lose her self-consciousness.

Perhaps my story is a trivial tale to make a pertinent point. But it's true that we need to understand that having confidence is not just about *us*. Not only because we appear more confident when self-consciousness disappears, but because *true confidence* is ultimately not 'me'-centred or 'me'-focused but God-centred and 'others'-focused.

In this chapter we're going to consider two friends of Jesus, whose natural confidence (given in very different measure) was transformed by God – in very different ways. They both shared an experience of the way in which God uses the confidence He gives us – for the benefit (even life-saving) of others and for the fulfilment of His plan.

Peter: a man transformed

If ever there were a man in need of a confidence overhaul, it was Peter. Surely commonly known as 'Peter-put-your-foot-in-it', this poor man hardly had the reputation of someone who got it right. A fisherman, impulsive by nature, he was sometimes an argumentative and tactless companion until, lacking in boldness and crippled by fear, he betrayed his dearest friend and Master. Broken, bewildered and wondering what on earth he could do to redeem the mess he'd made, he realised finally that redemption was not up to him – but up to Jesus. Wonderfully, despite and beneath it all, God recognised in Peter a heart of sincere faith.

Peter knew he'd blown it: God knew he could build on it. In that knowledge and relationship Peter began, at first, in continued fear and trembling, to lead the frail and apprehensive group of very human, yet believing, men and women who would become the Early Church. In Peter's case, it was perhaps his weakness and acknowledgement of inadequacy that enabled God to use him so powerfully; to fill him with the Holy Spirit and enable him to do amazing work that would have such a powerful personal impact on both individuals and large (and often hostile) crowds. The outpouring of the Holy Spirit fulfilled God's Word: 'No, this is what was spoken by the prophet Joel: "In the last days, God says, I will pour out my Spirit on all people"' (Acts 2:16–17).

The accounts in the book of Acts and elsewhere of the emergence and growth of the Early Church give us a glimpse of the power, joy and transforming delight of the promised and poured-out Holy Spirit – not to mention the resulting confidence in the believers. It's worth spending time immersing ourselves in these exciting accounts. They so clearly illustrate how God can move in breathtaking ways among the most weakened and broken individuals – and how He can work miracles with our confidence too.

Peter, the same bumbling, doubting, fear-filled and failing Peter we so identify with, is transformed into a bold, articulate speaker. With clarity, power and incredible confidence he shares a message that leads to the addition of 3,000 members to the Early Church: the result of the confidence and work of the Holy Spirit. Can this really be Peter? Can this really be the one who always seemed to get it wrong now so wonderfully getting it right? Yes, it is! Such is the wonderful – and downright hilarious – grace of God. Peter is transformed and inspired by the power of the Holy Spirit into a bold, uncompromising witness for Jesus and for God's plan for us all. 'Brothers, I can tell you confidently …' he says (Acts 2:29).

Peter's confident words are the result of three things: his knowledge and love of Jesus, his desire to share the message of salvation, and the power and witness of the Holy Spirit. The Holy Spirit is, in the real sense of the word, inspirational. Peter's words are so full of impact, so personal and so convincing that the people want to act upon them. Those who hear Peter don't just sit there, they *DO* something (Acts 2:36–41). In fact, in verse 37 we're told: 'they … said to Peter and the other apostles, "Brothers what shall we do?"' Those who were listening to Peter were moved by the Holy Spirit – and the impact was amazing. They were 'cut to the heart' (v.37). How often can *we* say that of our response to a sermon?!

As Peter's audience listen to his words they recognise the truth of the gospel: the Holy Spirit opens their eyes and they know they must respond. Peter immediately tells them how: 'Repent,' he says, 'be baptised and you will receive forgiveness and the gift of the Holy Spirit.' In the best marketing terms he outlines the action – but he also explains the benefits! It's clear that the Holy Spirit was an essential part of the lives of these new Christians from the very beginning. Their relationship with Him was fundamental. Peter wants them to be equipped, inspired and confident in their faith. The Holy Spirit offers the way.

When we try to live our Christian lives under our own steam, we will always end up burning out, becoming discouraged or losing our focus. Our relationship with the Holy Spirit is as fundamental as it was to Peter's new converts. Perhaps we forget that in a Western world so supported by technology and the idols of convenience.

Peter's Spirit-inspired message was heard and acted

upon. Both individually and corporately, that small group of bewildered followers began to grow in confidence: *true confidence*, Spirit-inspired confidence. It was confidence built on the acknowledged love of a Father, the fulfilled promises of a Saviour and the power of a promised Counsellor and Helper.

By the time we reach chapter 10 of the book of Acts, Peter has established a dynamic Church that has attracted controversy and drawn persecution upon itself, scattering its number far and wide. Peter arrives at Cornelius's house and speaks boldly to the friends and family who've gathered there to hear him (Acts 10:34–48). Peter gives us not just another great piece of oratory, but a template for what we would now call an 'evangelistic sermon' – sharing the gospel in a nutshell. He begins by affirming his knowledge that God's message is for everyone who will hear it. Then he picks up on what his audience already knows: what they have seen and heard about the work and witness of Jesus. Peter explains that Jesus 'went around doing good' in the power of the Holy Spirit, anointed by God the Father; he reminds his audience of Jesus' resurrection and of his own commission to share the gospel. Then, after a clear invitation – that all those who believe in Jesus' name will know forgiveness – the Holy Spirit steps in, taking over where Peter had (almost) left off.

This is a wonderful assurance for us. We may not be called to preach an evangelistic sermon; we may cringe at the thought of openly sharing our faith with others, no matter how much we long for them to know Jesus. But these verses give us confidence to do both. Not because we will necessarily come out with a message as eloquent and succinct as Peter's, but because God will always honour our heartfelt desire. He will send the Holy Spirit to 'take over' where we have 'left off' – even if that's after the first three words! This is the time for confidence not to be 'me'-focused but centred on God and focused on others. Telling a friend, work colleague or neighbour about the reality of our faith is never a conversation between only two people. When we ask the Holy Spirit to be present He will be; we can be confident of that.

Jesus 'went around doing good' in the power of the Holy Spirit. Peter testified to that in the same power by sharing his faith. Now it's over to you. The next time you sit down for a coffee with a friend, strike up a conversation on the bus or get chatting in the supermarket queue, who knows what He will bring to your conversation?

The woman at the well: a life-changing meeting

The Gospel of John gives us an account of one of the most intriguing meetings of Jesus' earthly ministry (John 4:4–42). The story of the woman at the well has come to mean much to me over the last year or two, and every time I look at it I notice a detail I missed before – or am struck by an impression somehow hidden between the lines.

We need to begin by reminding ourselves why this meeting was so remarkable. At first glance, neither the behaviour of Jesus nor that of the woman carrying the water jar seem particularly shocking to us. They are simply passing the time of day. But Jesus' behaviour would have been disturbing to any onlooker on three counts: the first relating to sex, the second to race and the third to reputation.

In Britain today we are largely a multicultural society where women are generally (if not universally) considered 'equal if different' to men. But rabbinic law in Jesus' day taught that a man must not talk to, or look at, a woman on the street – even if she were his sister or his wife. It just 'wasn't done'!

Culturally, Jews did not associate with Samaritans, the people of the northern kingdom of Israel, named after its capital city, Samaria. Their estrangement was borne out of complex and historical events. Samaritans were despised by the Jews because of their much earlier intermarriage with Gentiles, which followed the fall of the northern kingdom in 721 BC and the resettlement that resulted. The Jews considered that the Samaritans had 'watered down' their Jewish faith and so destroyed a temple that the Samaritans had built on Mount Gerizim. The Samaritan scriptures contained only the Pentateuch, the first five books of the Old Testament. So, although the Samaritans longed for and expected a Messiah, they knew little about Him.

By Jesus' time the feud between Jews and Samaritans had become bitter and entrenched. Yet, strangely, in the New Testament, it is the Samaritans who are so often open and receptive to the gospel.

Thirdly, there was this woman's reputation. She would probably assume that Jesus was a local man who knew all about her promiscuous lifestyle. Doubtless she approached the well expecting to fill her jar and walk away, suffering little more than the kind of look men usually gave her, knowing her reputation. She certainly didn't expect Jesus to strike up a conversation – and a life-changing one at that. Men like Him simply didn't talk to women like her. Indeed, in her confusion and alarm at His opening words, she more or less tells Him so!

As their conversation unfolds, she boldly asks Him who He is and her feistiness and confidence means that their conversation soon becomes deeper than the well itself.

We can only imagine what she is thinking as she listens to Jesus' words about water and life. We might assume from her response that she has failed to understand their metaphorical nature. At first it seems that she is thinking only of the physical and mundane rather than the spiritual and life-changing. She is just having a moan about all she has to do each day. But I think that may all be bluff and nonsense – a bit of fishwifery in the face of something bigger than she can cope with – avoidance tactics maybe. She's not accustomed to having her forthright comments handled in such a gentle and gracious way. She's used to dealing with men and their clever words – but this man unnerves her. What is He about? It's not long before she finds herself, knowingly or otherwise, on the very, breath-holding edge of Spirit-inspired insight and understanding – and about to make a giant leap of faith. With honesty and directness, Jesus meets her at the deepest point of her need; a need for saving grace and a longing to be known, loved and accepted for herself.

With a slightly trick question about husbands, Jesus takes a bolder step closer. He needs to establish real honesty if He is going to bring real life into this conversation. The woman's reply is evasive, but truthful. What He says is true. She recognises His insight as prophetic and links it to her own faith history. She longs to worship, she says, but her confidence is too much in the tradition and place of her people, not in the omnipotence of a living God. Jesus goes on to give her a picture of true worship as He prepares to introduce Himself as the Messiah. He has seen in her someone who will have the confidence to worship in honesty and truth, just as the Father requires.

Even before the woman recognises Jesus, she is bold and certain in her faith. She does not say 'I have heard', 'We have been told' or even 'It is written', but 'I know': 'I *know* that Messiah … is coming' (John 4:25, italics mine). This is the moment Jesus has been waiting for. Now He can introduce Himself. Using words that reflect the great 'I Am' He says, 'I who speak to you am he' (v.26). I wonder if she dropped her water jar in amazement – because she certainly left it behind in her hurry! Perhaps carrying it would have slowed her down, because she doesn't just leap into faith – she runs with it! Did Jesus smile wryly at her rapid faith-filled departure, I wonder? In a few dozen breathless paces between the well and the village this feisty, intelligent woman finds a new confidence and, on the way, she is transformed from a nameless water-drawer to a powerful witness!

The people to whom she ran with her story wouldn't normally want to associate with her, let alone go with her to meet a man she'd told them so much about. But, not only do they listen to her, they also do what she says – so confident and convincing is her faith. She demonstrates the heart of evangelism – faith in action through compassion: a compassion born out of a difficult life filled with difficult needs. Her faith prompts her to discern needs in the lives of others and to offer an encounter with Jesus as a way to meet those needs.

Her lifestyle was well known by everyone in the village. Yet, in telling others about Jesus' knowledge of that lifestyle, she is acknowledging that His salvation is greater than her sin. Her neighbours were amazed. Knowing the woman (and before they even meet Jesus, John says) they believed in Jesus 'because of the woman's testimony'. She had understood very quickly that true faith-filled confidence is not about 'me' but about others. Having received Jesus herself she set out, immediately, to share Him with other people.

Quite simply, in a moment of faith, this woman swapped the kind of confidence the world reveres for the kind of confidence that God rewards. I wonder if it was more a harnessing of confidence in the right direction than a swap – because God loves to powerfully use the raw material He sees in us when we allow Him to.

This woman had approached Jesus as a wounded woman: one whose brash and obvious confidence was based on a survival instinct – a way to be as a woman in a man's world. It was confidence that said: 'I can give as good as I get. Don't mess with me!' She was not afraid to challenge Jesus, nor to question and debate – something taboo for a woman, let alone a Samaritan woman. But as she spoke to Jesus it became apparent that hidden behind that brash exterior was her vulnerability. She did have some confidence – and Jesus was delighted to discover that it was a confidence in faith. A faith bound in tradition and heritage it's true, but within that faith He spotted a way to transform it into a faith that was personal. He saw, within her, the potential of a true worshipper, one whose confidence could (and would) be in the living God alone.

In a moment of recognition, a new confidence was released in her. It flooded her fear and apprehension, even her shame, to such an extent that she was able to share with others her certainty and assurance of who Jesus was. Even those who'd been the last to listen and the first to condemn couldn't ignore her confident witness. They also saw the way in which her brash boldness had been transformed by the touch of Jesus and the power of the Holy Spirit. Her confident, 'I must tell you!' faith was simply irresistible.

Peter and the woman at the well could not have been more different as people – either in themselves or to each other – before being met and changed by Jesus. One was a man, the other a woman; one a friend of Jesus, the other a forbidden acquaintance. Both experienced a transformation that enabled them to be confident – because their priority became not themselves, but what God could do for others through them. They took their eyes off 'me' and focused on 'others'.

Peter, so often impetuous, outspoken – the one who 'messed

up' – was not a man you'd want in a crisis! Yet Peter is powerfully transformed into a bold and confident communicator, trusted by God as a messenger of the gospel, speaking to thousands of complete strangers about God's love.

The Samaritan woman, once so sure, so brittle, so bruised by bravado (and by life) that even her neighbours rejected her, ends up sharing her life and its transformation with the very people who'd despised her – and with wonderful results.

An ordinary man and an ordinary woman, made extraordinary by the confidence of the Holy Spirit received through an encounter with Jesus, powerfully, and in very different ways, 'passed it on'.

So, what are we waiting for?!

True confidence:
if it was good enough for them ...

What are the practical implications of these biblical accounts for us as we grapple with issues of *true confidence* that 'isn't about me'?

I wish I could tell you that if you pray like Peter tomorrow you'll preach like him the day after. Or that being bold in faith like the woman at the well will have most of your 'village' following you to church. Of course I can't tell you that – but I know that, with God, all things are possible and that He *can*!

But faith rarely gives us an instant result or easy answer to any situation or question – whether it is 'others'-focused or not. Instead, our faith must go hand in hand with obedience, hope, humility and a willingness to be used as God chooses and according to our gifts. And, as a bonus, I believe that God likes confidence in Him to be *fun*! Confident others-focused faith comes from a confidence in a loving, giving, *exciting* God.

There should be no distinction between our 'ministry' – the

things we do for God and, with Him, for others – our everyday personal lives, our church lives or our community roles. Our lives lived for God should be seamless. But, in the light of these two stories, there are ways in which we can begin to explore confident others-focused faith in the different, albeit seamless, contexts of our own lives.

True confidence and personal faith – it's not about me

Firstly, both Peter and the woman demonstrated that God is a God of the second chance … and very often the third, fourth and fifth chance too. It's never too late for God to use us. We are never too messed up, too weak, too damaged or too inarticulate. God loves turning things around in our lives and turning the world upside down through us.

Secondly, out of their own encounters with Jesus, these two people discovered a passion to communicate, to share their stories and to give away the love they'd received. The priority, even of their personal faith, was other people.

Thirdly, they relied on the Person of Jesus not on themselves. Peter knew his failings and weaknesses and that he had let his Master down in the past. But he also knew that because of those weaknesses he could go nowhere else for the power and enabling he needed – except to Jesus. To depend on His Holy Spirit day to day, crowd to crowd, miracle to miracle.

The woman met Jesus on an ordinary day, in an ordinary way, going about her daily business. Yet, even in the midst of those chores, she was searching. God honoured her faith-filled search wonderfully as, in the span of a conversation, she grew close to Jesus. She asked questions, challenged, listened, hung on His every word and was honest about her doubts as well as her faith. I think Jesus honours that. On reflection I think that she may not have dropped her water jar in amazement or left it because it was too heavy, or even because the living water Jesus promised would be enough. Did she perhaps leave it because she knew that she would come back? Back to sit at His feet to hear more of His teaching – knowing that He would welcome her.

Peter and the woman both knew that Jesus was the source of life and faith and that 'In him and through faith in him we may approach God with freedom and confidence' (Eph. 3:12).

True confidence – it's given for the Church but it's not about us

Church is often the toughest place to have confidence, isn't it? There's always someone who seems to have more than us: the apparently doubt-less prayers; those who waft into church on Sunday morning on a spiritual high while we're wondering what we're doing there at all. At the same time, for all our inadequacies, there is so much we long to do and be within the Body of Christ. Yet we so often feel like the very littlest of little toes – and a calloused one at that!

Peter knew that he couldn't do any of the 'church stuff' on his own. He needed the Holy Spirit's guidance and inspiration. It was his very willingness to serve, his obedience and his acknowledgement of his own weaknesses that made him so open to the Holy Spirit. The work he had to do was not about him, Peter, but about other people – and about what God wanted for them.

It didn't matter that he wasn't word perfect, that his knees knocked as he stood up to talk or that some of the crowd heckled from the back. It was God's message and God's method – that was all that mattered. Paul knew that too: 'Such confidence as this is ours through Christ before God.

Not that we are competent in ourselves to claim anything for ourselves, but our competence comes from God. He has made us competent as ministers of a new covenant … of the Spirit … the Spirit gives life' (2 Cor. 3:4–6).

The woman at the well actually founded her own group of believers – going to her own people to share all she had heard and bringing them to Jesus for a kind of 'Foundations of Faith' mini-conference!

Often the hardest place to teach, share or witness is with our 'own people', whether within our own family or our church family. They know us, don't they! But the woman at the well knew that her 'own people' knew all about her – and it didn't matter. Her faith was above all that. Honest in her approach, there was an urgency that transcended everything else – and it was powerful.

The more we can be honest about our faith and our failings the more we can become a genuine body of believers, living in confidence alongside each another.

True confidence – it transforms the community when it's all about the world

Both Peter and the woman looked beyond their small corner. Peter was about to found a worldwide Church; the woman a village faith community – a big difference that mattered little. What was important was their immediate concern for the wider community, the bigger picture. It wasn't just about 'me' or even 'us'.

It is said that the Church is the only organisation that doesn't exist (or shouldn't exist) primarily for the benefit of its members. Yet, so often, our church gatherings seem little more than a social club with God as absent chairman. We shouldn't be closing our doors to think about how we bring people in, but putting on our coats and opening the doors in order to go out. Our work should be community-based not pew-bound. We should go where the people are.

Jesus spent time with people in conversation, demonstrating His concern, compassion and, sometimes, challenge. Faith-filled confidence that's 'not about us' should take us out into the community. Not in order to arrogantly further our 'evangelism project', or to publicise our church or our way of doing things as being the best. Instead, we should be there to relate, love, support, empower, get our hands dirty and show, practically, the love of Jesus and the difference it makes beyond the church door. That's 'not-about-me' *true confidence* in action.

Ask yourself
- How confidently do I approach Jesus? What do I expect Him to ask me?

- Do I believe in a God of the second, third and fourth chance?

- If so, what is the heart of the message that my belief in a 'God of the second chance' might give to others?

- Peter stood where the people were; the woman ran to find them. How does that challenge me to be confident in my faith?

For reflection

· ·

> I am still confident of this:
> > I will see the goodness of the LORD
> > in the land of the living.
> Wait for the LORD;
> > be strong and take heart
> > and wait for the LORD.

Psalm 27:13–14

What is the relationship between 'waiting' and 'confidence'?

Prayer

Father, whether I am a Peter or a woman with a water jar, I know that You long for me to approach You – and speak for You – 'in confidence'. Call me to You today, that I may stand before You knowing what true confidence *really is – and pass it on. Amen.*

Chapter 6

True confidence is …
about faith not feeling

*'So do not throw away your confidence; it will be richly
rewarded. You need to persevere so that when you have done the
will of God, you will receive what he has promised.'*
Hebrews 10:35–36

At the very beginning of this book, we looked at the definition of confidence and considered that, as Christians, the source of our confidence is best found in God, rather than in ourselves, our achievements or our status. Quite simply, it is better to have faith in God than in 'me' and to allow Him to give me self-worth that lasts because it is based on intimate relationship with Him.

The problem with having faith in ourselves is that we tend to construct our confidence on rather shaky foundations: the praise of others, the sharp business suit, getting the deal or – and most especially – our feelings.

It is, undoubtedly, great to 'feel' confident. On days when life is going well: we've just got a promotion, the car starts first time or the icing hasn't slid off the cake onto the plate as it usually does, we will 'feel' confident. But *true confidence* doesn't depend on what we feel; it depends on who we are, where we are, what we are and where we are going.

In this final chapter we will distil all we have learnt into a list of ingredients –a practical recipe – for confident living that we can live, work and worship with on a daily basis. That recipe should remind us of all we have discovered: that *true confidence* (even on those days when the car *doesn't* start and the icing *does* slide off the cake) depends on a sure foundation in God. That foundation consists of three Rs, three Fs and a genuine W! First in the confidence pot, the three Rs: not 'riting, reading and 'rithmetic, but roots, royalty and responsibility.

Roots

Please read the passage that follows and let it fill your heart as you read:

> I pray that out of his glorious riches he may strengthen you
> with power through his Spirit in your inner being, so that
> Christ may dwell in your hearts through faith. And I pray
> that you, being rooted and established in love, may have
> power, together with all the saints, to grasp how wide and
> long and high and deep is the love of Christ, and to know this
> love that surpasses knowledge – that you may be filled to the
> measure of all the fullness of God.
>
> Ephesians 3:16–19

For me this passage sums up what we need for the foundations
– the 'roots' – of *true confidence*. Paul tell us that the love of
God gives us the roots we need to grow in faith. Through
those roots, everything we need to be confident 'seeps' up
into our being. Do you remember Jeremiah's words about the
well-watered tree we considered in Chapter One? Here, Paul
parallels them New Testament style. So what do these verses
assure us of?

Firstly riches: God 'finances' our confidence. He gives
us all the resources we need to live a life of faith-filled
confidence – the power and indwelling of the Holy Spirit and
the example and 'indwelling' of Jesus. Paul is praying that
once we begin to know the strength of God's love for us and
are rooted in it, we will go on knowing and drawing on that
love. We will continue feeding on it through our 'roots' until
we are full up – until we are blossoming, if you like, with His
love. This is a love, he reminds us, that we can never know
or understand fully – there's just too much of it. We cannot
plumb the depths of God's love – it's limitless. His love is a
resource that we can continue drawing on forever: it never
runs out. This doesn't mean, of course, that we will always
feel strongly rooted in faith or full of blossoming confidence

like that riverside tree in Jeremiah (Jer. 17). Some days we will *feel* more like wilting than blossoming! But that's OK! Very simply, it's up to us to ask God, with sincere hearts and an honest assessment of our needs, for the resources we need to grow and blossom – remembering that confidence based on fact and faith is neither indicated by nor reliant on our feelings – wilting or otherwise!

Relationship

Secondly, *true confidence* is built on our relationship with God.

Our earthly relationships may contribute something similar to our confidence. If we know that someone believes in us, wants the best and will be there for us, we can have confidence – not just in that relationship, but in all our forays into the outside world. But human relationships are fallible; subject to conditional love; vulnerable to pressure. Our relationship with God depends on nothing more than our willingness to stand before Him just as we are: He is faithful, loves us unconditionally and doesn't give up on us. He gave His Son to close the gap we'd made through living life our own way (out of relationship with Him) and He longs for an honest and intimate relationship with us. You might remember that I said earlier that sometimes He even 'chases' us through life, in order that we might know that relationship.

A fellow church member was involved in the life of our church for nearly forty years before she understood what a relationship with Father God meant. She'd been involved in almost every area of church life, but saw God as a distant figure to be worshipped on Sunday and obeyed. It took a very tender encounter with God as Father for her to understand that, whilst corporate worship and obedience are important, what God really wanted was a close relationship with her. Her faith was transformed! She became like a giggly little girl – fresh from sitting on the lap of a safe and loving Father!

Knowing God in relationship means that we have been given amazing privileges that add to our confidence: we are heirs of His kingdom with Jesus (Rom. 8:17); we have royal status and we are part of one family (Eph 4:3–6). But with that privilege of relationship comes responsibility, both for ourselves and for others.

Responsibility

Confidence comes from doing as well as being.

CEOs of large companies often work with interns who shadow the boss and learn something about their role 'on the job'. I once worked with an organisation whose CEO would frequently drop his interns in at the deep end where tasks were concerned. 'You can do it!' he would say – and walk out of the room, leaving them with their jaws dropped. To him it seemed best simply to give them the job to do rather than tell them how to do it. The interns didn't always thank him for this and things didn't always go smoothly! But, very quickly, they learned not only responsibility in getting the job done, but also grew enormously in confidence. They realised that they could do it and that their work was making a valuable contribution to the organisation. Best of all, they had the praise and approval of the boss.

Christian responsibility is about faith in action. Our responsibility as heirs is one we share with Jesus. We're to be responsible for our own actions in 'getting the job done', but we are also to share responsibility for the less able and more vulnerable amongst us.

Chapter 58 of Isaiah teaches us what God requires from us, as far as responsibility for others is concerned. In verses 6 to 14 we are reminded that we are to serve the weak, the broken, the poor and the marginalised:

> ... and if you spend yourselves on behalf of the hungry and
> satisfy the needs of the oppressed, then your light will rise in
> the darkness, and your night will become like noonday.
>
> Isaiah 58:10

Not only do we bless those we serve when we put faith into action, but we bring blessing on ourselves in fulfilling our responsibilities.

Jesus, as our role model, was fully focused on the work His Father had sent Him to do. He was not concerned with building up His reputation or being seen in the right places with the right people. (He was usually seen in the 'wrong' places with the 'wrong' people!) He did not rely on outward props, public acclaim or status. Instead He was focused, prayerful, compassionate and often challenging, and He pointed the way to the Father in everything He did. He was confident in what He had been given to do and in the Person who would give Him the resources with which to do it.

Confidence is not about 'me' but it can be found in doing the work God wants us to do; in forgetting ourselves and 'spending' ourselves on behalf of others.

Next we add the three Fs of *true confidence* ...

Fearlessness

> After they prayed, the place where they were meeting was
> shaken. And they were all filled with the Holy Spirit and
> spoke the word of God boldly.
>
> Acts 4:31

There is a thin and dangerous piece of ground to be navigated between fearlessness and stupidity! Peter, as we have discovered, knew both sides of that piece of ground – and we should be aware of the boundary line too. But in the early chapters of Acts he and his companions are different men – and women – empowered by the Holy Spirit to do the work God has given them to do. They are fearless, knowing that God is their ultimate security, their ultimate confidence.

God had given Peter and his friends a very special gift of power and enabling through His Holy Spirit. It was a public, as well as a personal, transformation – not, primarily, for their personal benefit but for the benefit of those who needed to know God. We may feel that this kind of empowering is not for us today: but it can be. When all else fails us (our confidence included) God doesn't.

The key here is our willingness and our heart. We may not feel able to do the work God has given us to do; to start the conversation we know He wants us to initiate; to go to the less safe parts of our city to live and work. But if our heart burns with a passion to be His hands, feet and voice and to follow His leading, He *will* do the enabling. God keeps *His* promises. So often it isn't fear of physical danger that holds us back, but fear of what others will think; fear of making a fool of ourselves: a very common manifestation of lack of confidence. I believe (from my own experience) that God will quickly find someone else to do the work or say the word if we are held back by such self-consciousness. The disappointment that results when we see that happen can be heartbreaking.

Earlier, I told the story of my participation (or rather non-participation) in a creative development meeting with some very gifted and experienced leaders: the movers and shakers in their field. As I left that meeting having contributed little, my friend and colleague scolded me for not taking a more active part: 'You have so much to offer that is relevant!' he said. 'Why didn't you?' I explained that I felt overawed by everyone who was there. 'They are so gifted and so experienced,' I said feebly. 'I couldn't possibly be on a par with them!' 'Then why,' said my friend, 'were you asked to be one of them?'

Thankfully, as we have discovered, God is the God of the second, third and fourth chance. He will keep on giving us the opportunity to be fearless for Him when we ask – we just need to be bold!

On more than a couple of (hundred!) occasions since that day I have had to ask God to make me bold, simply because I didn't want to miss out on doing His will, on giving Him glory and knowing His pleasure. Thankfully, He does.

What's more important: not losing *our* face or not missing the smile on His?

Faith

Faith is defined in *The NIV Thematic Study Bible* as:

A constant outlook of trust towards God, whereby human beings abandon all reliance on their own efforts and put their full confidence in him, his words and his promises.[1]

In abandoning confidence in ourselves we can have confidence in God – and confidence, whatever happens. True faith is faith *whatever*.

Some of us may panic slightly at the idea of 'abandonment'. But in asking us to abandon self-reliance God is not wanting to turn us into wet blankets with no decision-making abilities or 'Yes-men' and 'Yes-women' without freedom. Instead He wants to liberate us from the way in which self-reliance closes the door to His provision, His comfort and His empowering. Relying on self often means that we also rely on circumstances and our feelings about them. But faith transcends circumstances and goes beyond feelings. We are asked to maintain that 'constant outlook of trust' whatever befalls us and whatever we feel. No one is saying that's easy: sometimes it will be the most difficult thing we've ever been asked to do. But remembering that faith is based on fact – the fact of God's plan, the reality of Jesus' mission and the promise of eternal life – and not on feeling, gives us a much stronger foundation on which to build our confidence. To make that faith work on a daily basis we have to find ways to weave its reality into our every waking moment. That's not easy either! But it is possible and some days it will be easier than others.

There is nothing automatic or neatly polished about living a life of faith with Jesus on a daily basis. It can be a messy, often discouraging and frequently frustrating business – and we ought to admit that to each other more often. But underpinning our messy, often discouraging and frequently frustrating life of faith there is a promise. It's a promise that, if we're honest, we don't quite understand. It has a mystical quality and a sense of the unknown. But it's a promise that offers a mere glimpse of something wonderful that we can scarcely imagine – and it imbues us with hope. Hope that on bad days may be like that flickering flame of faith I mentioned earlier, subject to every breeze of disappointment and puff of exasperation. But it is there, nonetheless.

Paul lived a life founded on that kind of faith and it's Paul who writes about it: Faith is 'being sure of what we hope for and certain of what we do not see' (Heb. 11:1). Hebrews 11 gives us a wonderful platform from which to consider the nature of that 'glimpse of something wonderful' faith – read it if you have time. It's a great confidence booster!

Future

Our faith is founded on hope in a God who holds – indeed who *is* – the future. Sadly, the state of our world leaves many with little hope. For some, the future is empty, lacking in promise. When asked what they fear most many will say 'the future'. That fear is often contained in the unknown element of what lies ahead.

Christians have an incredible responsibility in the face of such anxiety. It is too easy for us to flippantly present our hope as 'pie in the sky when you die', which has little relevance to the reality of most people's daily struggle. What we need to present, and model, is a God, a relationship, a community – and a kingdom – that begins now. A human God who identifies with suffering; a safe and secure relationship with a Father God that has relevance for today in preparation for tomorrow. We need also to model a community that gives real, reliable, love and support and doesn't use sticking plasters of platitude; a kingdom that offers peace and certainty, right at this moment – not just something airy-fairy resembling a spiritual lifeboat in a sea of uncertainty. People without hope need to know that God is real – and that He holds their past, their present and their future: that God is our only certainty.

Just this morning I took part in a radio interview about my experience of cancer. The interviewer asked me how I lived with the 'uncertainty' of the future. As this was a Christian radio station the question seemed rather odd! Of course I understood what the interviewer meant: she was asking how I live with not knowing what might happen tomorrow and whether the cancer might come back. Rather unfairly, perhaps,

I turned the tables and said something like the following: 'None of us know what will happen tomorrow, do we? But we do have one great certainty: a certainty in the future that stands big and bold and bright in front of whatever tomorrow, this afternoon or even the next half-hour holds. Our certainty is that although we don't know what the future holds we know who holds the future. God Himself. He is certain – and that's all I need to know.'

Knowing what we have now – a relationship with God; security and significance in His sight – carries us forward through whatever our earthly future may have in store for us. (Remember, Paul was convinced: 'Nothing can separate us from the love of God.') It carries us to what we are clearly told our eternal future promises: heaven, a secure inheritance and an eternity safe in the presence of a Father God. Jesus told us: 'In my Father's house are many rooms; if it were not so, I would have told you. I am going there to prepare a place for you' (John 14:2). 'We have this hope', says the writer of Hebrews, 'as an anchor for the soul, firm and secure' (Heb. 6:19).

God is Lord of the past, present and future – of that we can be confident.

And last, but definitely not least, we add the big heartfelt W ...

Worship

You may remember that the nature of worship was a key element in Jesus' conversation with the woman at the well. He recognised in her the honesty of a true worshipper, one who worships in spirit and in truth: 'God is spirit and his worshippers must worship in spirit and in truth' (John 4:24).

As I have neared the end of the journey of writing this book I have recognised a key link between confidence and worship. It's in true worship that we are freed from all sense of incompetence, failure and inadequacy – past, present or future. It's in true worship that we stand before God in perfect intimacy. He always sees us just as we are, but in moments of true worship I think we begin to see ourselves as He sees us and we catch just a tiny glimpse of His glory too. When we worship God we can know true freedom – and in that freedom there is confidence:

> Now the Lord is the Spirit, and where the Spirit of the
> Lord is, there is freedom. And we, who with unveiled faces
> all reflect [or contemplate] the Lord's glory, are being
> transformed into his likeness with ever-increasing glory,
> which comes from the Lord, who is the Spirit.
>
> 2 Corinthians 3:17–18

The more we contemplate God in worship, the more we reflect His likeness. As we do so, He transforms each one of us into the person we are truly meant to be: the unique person of His design, made in His image; a person He loves and values and draws to Himself, but also someone He 'sends out' to do His work in the world, equipped and empowered, with unique gifts; a person who is confident in His love and His leading and to whom He will one day say, 'Well done, good and faithful servant.' Understanding those facts can be both awe-inspiring and liberating.

While working on this book I was privileged to speak at a weekend away for a large group of women from a church in the south east of England. I am often asked to speak at such events, but long before the weekend arrived I had a sense that God would do something special. That can add something of a pressure – not just to the event, but also to the speaker! From the moment we met together there was only gentleness, warmth and the presence of God. Many of the women didn't know each other particularly well, but God did something amazing as He introduced these women to one another. Their fellowship, their laughter, their conversation, their tears, their heartfelt concern and prayer for one another's lives all bore God's hallmarks.

The verses on the previous page (from 2 Corinthians) were highlighted for us during the weekend, as we spent time exploring what *true confidence* means to God and to us and as I shared some of the material for this book. Our times of worship were sensitively planned. There was an increasing knowledge that we were standing before God as women who longed to love and serve Him more freely.

On the final morning I woke early, my heart bursting with what God might do that day. Unable to pray out loud in my room for fear of waking my neighbours (yes, my prayers were that urgent and fervent!), I went out to pace along a nearby farm track. I prayed loudly and tearfully that God would speak powerfully through me. I told Him that I loved these 'girls' already and that I wanted them to see more of the God who loved them so much more. I returned to my room a whole lot muddier, but with a renewed sense of expectation – even a commissioning.

While worshipping at the beginning of the morning session, I had the strong impression, just before I spoke, that God was saying to me, 'Take off your shoes: you are standing on Holy Ground.' Now, when you're the speaker and are standing at the front, you don't exactly want to do something to draw attention to yourself – least of all remove your shoes! But again, God said, 'Take off your shoes: you are standing on holy ground.' I could not refuse. I slipped out of my shoes and stood before God in worship. The room became hushed as we stood in silence, knowing the gentle and powerful presence of the Holy Spirit. When I walked up to speak a few minutes later I felt as if I were fired by an internal jet engine! But I also knew a sense of quiet awe and wonder. God gave me the words – and how! I felt as if He had ridden out across the heavens on every one – laughing as He went!

Later, in an effort to understand God's 'barefoot' directions, I read the stories of Moses and Joshua, both of whom were asked to remove their shoes with those same words. I realised that they'd been asked to do so because they were in the presence of God and were about to be commissioned to do a special task for Him. God had been with us powerfully that morning. We had stood with 'unveiled faces', contemplating Him, and He had blessed us – and, in some cases, commissioned us. We had known what it was, just for a few moments, to 'worship in spirit and in truth'. What freedom and confidence there was in that intimate worship! I believe God was saying that we would find a vital source of *true confidence* as we worshipped Him. And we did.

There is nowhere better to stand and know *true confidence* than before God in true worship. Worship in spirit and in truth with 'unveiled' faces brings freedom.

Perhaps a word about worship should really have come at the beginning of this book as we focused firstly on God. Yet, if to stand (or sit) before God in worship is to know true acceptance, freedom and confidence, it can take a journey such as we've travelled in this book to reach that point. I hope that we are now at a place of rest and promise, as well as of worship. So I've placed these thoughts on worship here.

As we reach this resting place, I pray that we are also being prepared for a new and confident walk with God. Worship seems to me to be a great place to start.

So, in a time of final reflection, let's spend some time worshipping God before we pray this prayer.

Amazing God
As I stand before you, face unveiled,
I may only glimpse Your glory.
Nothing in my imagination prepares me
for the wonder of You, Lord.
But I know that You call me here to this place
where I now stand or sit,
chin uplifted, arms outstretched, barefoot perhaps –
for wherever I am standing
this is Holy Ground.

As I contemplate how much You love me –
fill me with confidence.
As I try to measure how much You have done for me –
fill me with confidence.
As I bring my past, my present and my future before You –
fill me with confidence.

Father God, I know that there is no greater thing
I can do on earth, but serve You.
Take my heart, my soul, my hands, my feet,
my voice, my gifts and my talents
and infuse them with Your power,
Your love and Your enabling.
Remind me of my value in Your sight
and my responsibility to others.

But most of all, Lord God,
remind me of the daring, exciting, breathtaking ride
my life with You can be
when I know *true confidence*.

Lord, show me something today
to remind me that
this is just the beginning ...

1. *The NIV Thematic Study Bible* (London: Hodder and Stoughton, 1996) p.1813.

National Distributors

UK: (and countries not listed below)
CWR, Waverley Abbey House, Waverley Lane, Farnham, Surrey GU9 8EP.
Tel: (01252) 784700 Outside UK (44) 1252 784700

AUSTRALIA: CMC Australasia, PO Box 519, Belmont, Victoria 3216.
Tel: (03) 5241 3288 Fax: (03) 5241 3290

CANADA: David C Cook Distribution Canada, PO Box 98, 55 Woodslee Avenue, Paris, Ontario N3L 3E5.
Tel: 1800 263 2664

GHANA: Challenge Enterprises of Ghana, PO Box 5723, Accra.
Tel: (021) 222437/223249 Fax: (021) 226227

HONG KONG: Cross Communications Ltd, 1/F, 562A Nathan Road, Kowloon.
Tel: 2780 1188 Fax: 2770 6229

INDIA: Crystal Communications, 10-3-18/4/1, East Marredpalli, Secunderabad - 500026, Andhra Pradesh.
Tel/Fax: (040) 27737145

KENYA: Keswick Books and Gifts Ltd, PO Box 10242, Nairobi.
Tel: (02) 331692/226047 Fax: (02) 728557

MALAYSIA: Salvation Book Centre (M) Sdn Bhd, 23 Jalan SS 2/64, 47300 Petaling Jaya, Selangor.
Tel: (03) 78766411/78766797 Fax: (03) 78757066/78756360

NEW ZEALAND: CMC Australasia, PO Box 303298, North Harbour, Auckland 0751.
Tel: 0800 449 408 Fax: 0800 449 049

NIGERIA: FBFM, Helen Baugh House, 96 St Finbarr's College Road, Akoka, Lagos.
Tel: (01) 7747429/4700218/825775/827264

PHILIPPINES: OMF Literature Inc, 776 Boni Avenue, Mandaluyong City.
Tel: (02) 531 2183 Fax: (02) 531 1960

SINGAPORE: Alby Commercial Enterprises Pte Ltd, 95 Kallang Avenue #04-00, AIS Industrial Building, 339420.
Tel: (65) 629 27238 Fax: (65) 629 27235

SOUTH AFRICA: Struik Christian Books, 80 MacKenzie Street, PO Box 1144, Cape Town 8000.
Tel: (021) 462 4360 Fax: (021) 461 3612

SRI LANKA: Christombu Publications (Pvt) Ltd, Bartleet House, 65 Braybrooke Place, Colombo 2.
Tel: (9411) 2421073/2447665

TANZANIA: CLC Christian Book Centre, PO Box 1384, Mkwepu Street, Dar es Salaam.
Tel/Fax: (022) 2119439

USA: David C Cook Distribution Canada, PO Box 98, 55 Woodslee Avenue, Paris, Ontario N3L 3E5, Canada.
Tel: 1800 263 2664

ZIMBABWE: Word of Life Books (Pvt) Ltd, Christian Media Centre, 8 Aberdeen Road, Avondale, PO Box A480 Avondale, Harare. Tel: (04) 333355 or 091301188

For email addresses, visit the CWR website: www.cwr.org.uk

CWR is a Registered Charity – Number 294387

CWR is a Limited Company registered in England – Registration Number 1990308

Day and Residential Courses
Counselling Training
Leadership Development
Biblical Study Courses
Regional Seminars
Ministry to Women
Daily Devotionals
Books and Videos
Conference Centre

Trusted all Over the World

CWR HAS GAINED A WORLDWIDE
reputation as a centre of excellence for
Bible-based training and resources. From
our headquarters at Waverley Abbey
House, Farnham, England, we have been
serving God's people for over 40 years
with a vision to help apply God's Word
to everyday life and relationships. The
daily devotional *Every Day with Jesus* is
read by nearly a million readers an issue
in more than 150 countries, and our
unique courses in biblical studies and
pastoral care are respected all over the
world. Waverley Abbey House provides a
conference centre in a tranquil setting.

For free brochures on our seminars and
courses, conference facilities, or a catalogue
of CWR resources, please contact us at the
following address:
**CWR, Waverley Abbey House, Waverley
Lane, Farnham, Surrey GU9 8EP, UK**

Telephone: +44 (0)1252 784700
Email: mail@cwr.org.uk
Website: www.cwr.org.uk

 Applying God's Word
to everyday life and relationships

Other Inspiring Women Books:

Prepared for Spiritual Battle

Anne Le Tissier

Be emboldened to use your authority in Christ to defeat the enemy with this in-depth look at our spiritual armour as outlined in Ephesians 6.

112-page paperback
ISBN: 978-1-85345-471-4

Finding Freedom – The joy of surrender

Helena Wilkinson

Discover the deepest joy and freedom possible – through the grace of deep surrender – and gain a closer walk with God.

112-page paperback
ISBN: 978-1-85345-451-6

Created as a Woman

Beverley Shepherd

Takes a fresh look at what it means to be a woman and to have the Lord's unconditional and unchangeable love, through biblical insights, personal testimonies and the author's own life experiences.

112-page paperback
ISBN: 978-1-85345-450-9

Price: £6.99 each

Prices correct at time of printing and exclusive of p&p